—— LOST LINES:——

SOUTHERN

NIGEL WELBOURN

IAN ALLAN
Publishing

C O N T E N T S

First published 1996

ISBN 0 7110 2458 8

Published by Ian Allan Publishing, an imprint of Ian Allan Ltd, Terminal House,
Station Approach, Shepperton, Surrey TW17 8AS.
Printed by Ian Allan Printing Ltd, Coombelands House, Coombelands Lane,
Addlestone, Weybridge, Surrey KT15 1HY.

ACKNOWLEDGEMENTS

I would like to thank all those who helped me with this book.
In particular, I would like to thank my parents whose patience and understanding when I was
younger allowed me to visit so many lines that are now closed.
I would also like to thank all those courteous and helpful railwaymen and women who once
worked on the lines mentioned in this book.

Nigel P. Welbourn DIP TP, DIP TS, MRTPI, FRGS.

Cover pictures supplied courtesy of Colour-Rail.

Introduction

The Southern Region is covered in the fifth book in the series Lost Lines. A cross-section of closed lines has been selected for this volume, for their regional interest and for their wider historical and geographical associations.

In 1923, by amalgamation of smaller companies, the railways of Great Britain were grouped into the 'Big Four': the Southern Railway, the London & North Eastern Railway, the London Midland & Scottish Railway, and the Great Western Railway. When these private companies were nationalised on 1 January 1948, the new organisation — British Railways — was divided into six Regions for management purposes. A separate Southern Region was established, the others being the Scottish, London Midland, Eastern, Western and North Eastern Regions.

Although there had already been some closures, at their formation the six Regions covered one of the most comprehensive railway networks in the world. Yet it was clear, even then, that the changing trends in economic and travel patterns were not reflected in the distribution of lines. The problem was compounded in that after heavy use during World War 2, the equipment on many lines was life-expired. Thus it was that the railways at Nationalisation had extensive arrears of both maintenance and investment.

The ever-increasing inroads of the car and the lorry meant that financially the railways were no longer in a particularly sound position and British Railways fell ever deeper into debt. As a consequence, in the 1960s notice was served that the complete railway network, which had survived relatively intact until that time, would be scrutinised as never before. The financial contribution of individual lines was to be examined and it was clear, from the then somewhat stringent methods of accountancy, that many would be unlikely to survive on a purely commercial basis. In a surprisingly short time the system was reduced in size and, by the 1970s, when the brake was eventually applied on closures, about 8,000 miles over the whole system had been lost, a length of closed line equal to the diameter of the world.

In the knowledge that change was inevitable, I started in the 1960s to record my travels by train and eventually covered, with a few short exceptions, every passenger railway line on each of the six Regions. The railway network is now much smaller than when I first set out and indeed the Southern Region itself was abandoned after over four decades of geographical division in favour of other methods of organisation. My subsequent visits to lines closed show much still survives. Indeed, the earthworks and structures of abandoned lines have their own fascination, lost to the present, but certainly not forgotten.

Above: Map of the Regional Boundaries 1958.
Ian Allan Library

1 Historical perspective

It is of interest that although the Southern Region in later years developed predominantly as a passenger-carrying railway, the first railway in its hinterland was the mineral railway, the Surrey Iron Railway, which opened as far back as 1803. Nonetheless, one of the earliest passenger lines was also within the Southern Region. Pilgrims travelled from all over Europe to Canterbury and the first passenger route of the Southern Region can also be traced back to this town. The Canterbury & Whitstable Railway, opened in 1830, was the first steam-run passenger line in southern England and, in a foretaste of the future, was the first to issue season tickets. At the other end of the Region the Bodmin & Wadebridge Railway opened in 1834. This was followed in 1836 by the opening of the London & Greenwich Railway which was the first railway to enter London. From these short lines eventually a profusion of routes developed from London to Kent, the south coast and southwest, all later to become part of three well-known railway companies.

Below: The opening of most lines was a time for celebration. This view of the highly decorated Isle of Wight Central Railway 4-4-0T No 6 was taken at Merstone Junction in 1897, on the inauguration of the line from Newport to St Lawrence in the Isle of Wight. All routes to Merstone were closed by 1956. *Ian Allan Library*

The London & South Western Railway (LSWR) developed from the London & Southampton Railway and was the largest constituent of the Southern Railway. It ultimately ran services over about 1,000 miles of track from London Waterloo to Southampton, Bournemouth and Portsmouth. Its main line to the southwest, via Salisbury and Exeter, ran to Plymouth with branches extending to many coastal resorts including those on the Atlantic coast of Devon and Cornwall. The railway claimed to be 'the holiday line' and although it was sometimes unkindly nicknamed 'the Long & Slow Way Round', it was an efficient and businesslike railway, one of the first to use automatic signalling and developing an early 600V dc third rail electrification project in 1915. In the London area Waterloo station and the Feltham marshalling yard were the most modern in the metropolis and a substantial electric suburban traffic developed. Noted for its fine Adams-designed locomotives, in some respects the LSWR was the only real main line in the south.

The London Brighton & South Coast Railway (LBSCR) or 'The Brighton' as it was often called, ran from its two main terminals in London, at Victoria and London Bridge, to Brighton and the south coast. Routes also stretched to Newhaven and Hastings in the east and Portsmouth in the west. In the London area the railway was hit by competition from electric trams and was therefore early with its own electrification, starting a 6,600V ac overhead system in 1909.

Above: The Southern in the streets of London. The railway through Grove Street, Deptford, was built to the cattle market and docks in 1899. It became a military depot in 1915. Here a Southern Railway ex-LBSCR Class D1 0-4-2T No 2215 hauls a freight train from the depot past a Commer van. Maintenance of this street tramway was transferred from the Southern Railway to the War Office in 1927. This view was taken on 21 March 1940; the branch finally closed at the end of 1963. *Fox*

Below: Ramsgate Harbour station at the turn of the century. A 1,638yd tunnel led down to the terminus that was conveniently located for the beach. Rationalisation led to its closure by the Southern Railway in July 1926. Some of the structures associated with the station still remain. *Ian Allan Library*

The railway publicised its lines as elevated electric as opposed to the underground electric, effectively establishing the vast Southern Electric system. The main line to Brighton was particularly fine, with both the North and South Downs being penetrated by long tunnels. For many years locomotives bore a 'yellow' livery, called 'improved engine green', which was said by some to be the result of the LBSCR's Chief Mechanical Engineer, William Stroudley, being colour-blind.

The South Eastern & Chatham Railway (SECR) ran from its London termini at Victoria, Charing Cross, Cannon Street and Holborn Viaduct to destinations, particularly in Kent. For many years there had been bitter hostility between the two main components, the South Eastern Railway (SER) and the London Chatham and Dover Railway (LCDR). These two waged a long and expensive commercial war, which resulted in a number of duplicated lines and a large amount of money being wasted in a struggle which lasted for many decades, before a peace treaty in the form of the SECR was reached.

The SECR was enthusiastic about electrification and favoured a high voltage dc system with a

PENTIRE HEAD NEAR PADSTOW BY NORMAN WILKINSON. PI

NORTH CORNWALL
BY
SOUTHERN RAILWAY

Above: Not all closures date from the Beeching era. The Southern Railway looked carefully at the finances of secondary lines. This is a view of the derelict Bentworth & Lasham station, on the Basingstoke to Alton branch, which was closed to passengers by the Southern Railway in 1932 and to all traffic four years later. *Ian Allan Library*

Left: At the other extremity of the region from Ramsgate was Padstow. The Southern Railway was keen to promote the area covered by its routes and this painting of Pentire Head near Padstow, by Norman Wilkinson, was one of a series of landscape posters produced by the Railway. *Courtesy NRM*

protected live rail, but financial restraints and World War 1 prevented the implementation of this system. The railway provided important continental traffic and provided a 'Grande Vitesse' freight depot at Blackfriars. Even when merged into the Southern Railway the SECR was still not a single company, but the two separate SER and LCDR companies run by a managing committee.

No less than 14 subsidiary smaller companies were also absorbed into the Southern Railway. Many of these were historical anomalies which to all intents and purposes had long since been absorbed into larger railways. However, of particular distinction was the Somerset & Dorset Railway 'Swift & Delightful' which was shared with the Midland Railway, the Isle of Wight Railways and the famous Lynton & Barnstaple narrow gauge line.

The Southern Railway came into existence on 1 January 1923. Of the 'Big Four' railways so formed. the Southern was the smallest and for the first years the railway had to struggle with some very diverse and run-down assets. However, unlike many of the declining northern industrial areas, the Southern inherited growing commuter traffic and an increasing population. Consequently the railway was able to develop its clean and businesslike 'Southern Electric' passenger services which formed the basis of the present largely 750V dc electric third rail system.

Eventually the largest suburban electric network in the world developed. The increase in passengers after commuter lines were electrified was known as the 'sparks effect'. Although the Southern's decision to go for a third rail system has on occasions been criticised, after a decade of daily travelling 'under the wires' from Brentwood and a decade daily of travelling by third rail from Swanley, I can say that third rail is the winner on reliability — except in snowy conditions.

The Southern established a particularly strong corporate identity. It introduced regular clockface timings and a considerable number of modern stations. It also developed the large concrete production yard at Exmouth Junction which assembled a distinctive range of concrete railway equipment, much of which is still in use.

At its formation the Southern Railway had a monopoly on cross-Channel traffic and was a substantial dock owner. Its 'Atlantic Coast Express' ran to resorts like Ilfracombe, Bude and Padstow, whilst boat trains such as the 'Golden Arrow' and the 'Night Ferry', together with Pullman expresses such as the Devon, Brighton and Bournemouth 'Belles' became well known.

The railway promoted an image of leisure and holidays. It contracted out the management of its hotels. With some exceptions, these were located primarily at the London termini and at the main ports of Dover, Folkestone, Newhaven and Southampton with others at coastal locations such as Deal, Hythe and Sidmouth. Although some have since been demolished or put to alternative uses, and none are now in railway ownership, the hotels at Victoria, Charing Cross, Deal and Hythe remain open.

The locomotive works at Eastleigh, Ashford and Brighton produced under Maunsell and Bulleid a forward-looking and largely successful range of distinctive locomotives. So distinctive in Bulleid's case that the 'air smoothed' encased boilers of his Pacific class locomotives became known as 'Spam cans', and were amongst the last steam engines to survive in regular BR service.

Both World Wars had a massive impact on the railways in southern England. World War 2 had a great effect on the Southern Railway. Many railwaymen were killed and much damage was caused to buildings and equipment, including the loss of 12 ships.

Atlantic Coast Express

TO THE WEST OF ENGLAND FROM LONDON (WATERLOO) EVERY WEEKDAY AT 11 A.M.

ILFRACOMBE
5¼ HRS

BUDE
5¼ HRS

PADSTOW
6 HRS

EXETER
3¼ HRS

PLYMOUTH
5¼ HRS

FOR FURTHER INFORMATION PLEASE ENQUIRE AT STATIONS AND TRAVEL AGENTS

SOUTHERN
BRITISH RAILWAYS

Above: This former British Railways poster shows that many South West Coast resorts were once served by rail. *Courtesy NRM*

The coastal connections resulted in massive troop and equipment movements. The strains of World War 2 were to lead to nationalisation, but the Southern Railway was second only to the GWR in financial success. By the time the Southern was nationalised on 1 January 1948 there had been a considerable turn-around in its fortunes and it is perhaps not too surprising, therefore, that the first chairman of British Railways was a former Southern man.

After some years of nationalisation the Southern Region made improvements, including the long-awaited Kent Coast electrification. Yet just as this was completed there was growing financial concern and in 1963 the Reshaping Report, which became better known as the Beeching Report, was produced. The Southern Region had to offer up its share of cuts and non-electrified lines did not fare well in this report, but one of the many untoward recommendations was the proposed closure of all remaining lines on the Isle of Wight.

The Southern Region was cut down in size by a major boundary change at the end of 1962 which transferred the ex-Southern Railway lines west of Salisbury in the southwest and most of the former Somerset & Dorset line to the Western Region. Some of these former 'rival' lines appeared to have fared less successfully when it came to closures than the

Below: When this view of Holborn Viaduct was taken on 16 July 1960 the daily main line duty was still rostered for ex-SECR Class D1 4-4-0s. No 31489 is seen here with the 6.56am Holborn Viaduct parcels train which then formed the 7.24am London Bridge to Ramsgate train. *S. Creer*

ex-GWR lines already established with the Western Region. By the 1970s the distinctive Southern Region green livery had been converted to the blue and grey standard identity of British Rail and in 1991 the Southern Region itself disappeared in favour of other forms of management.

Yet the days of contraction are hopefully gone. A new main line — the Channel Tunnel rail link — is to cross Kent to the Channel Tunnel and it is generally agreed that the commuter lines into London, in spite of their substantial rush hour peaks, are critical to the success of the City. Yet off the beaten track, even in the most bustling parts of the south, many traces of abandoned tracks and the structures of lost lines can still be found.

Above: The first standard gauge preserved BR passenger line to be opened was in the former Southern Region. The Bluebell Railway has now been in operation since the early 1960s. Here memories of the early days are evoked by ex-North London Railway 0-6-0T pulling out of Horsted Keynes on 2 June 1962. *R. C. Riley*

Below: Most of the vast electric third rail London suburban system survived the cuts, although parts are in a poor state of repair, or used only at peak times, such as the main part of Crystal Palace Low Level station. This view of '4-SUB' units Nos 4108 and 4102 was taken at the station on 19 May 1972. Traces of the old overhead electrification system can still be seen on a number of lines in this area. *J. Scrace*

Below left: Holborn Viaduct was one of the few passenger terminal closures in central London. Opened in 1874, the last special train of Kent Coast '4-CEP' units left the terminus on 26 January 1990, after which the site was rapidly redeveloped. *Ian Allan Library*

2 Geography of the region

For the purposes of this book the boundaries selected are those of the Southern Region at Nationalisation as the area covered at that time was more coterminous with the old railway companies. Originally the Southern Region served an area from Ramsgate to Padstow, including the former London & South Western Railway routes to Plymouth and in Devon and Cornwall. However, in later boundary changes, the region was reduced in territorial area when the former Southern lines west of Salisbury were transferred to the Western Region.

In its final form the Southern Region comprised extensive suburban lines in south London and a series of routes that ran to all the major south coast resorts east of Weymouth. The lines that radiated from London cut through the North Downs gap towns of Basingstoke, Guildford, Redhill and Sevenoaks. The South Downs also presented physical difficulties for some lines in reaching the Sussex coast. Furthermore, when the region was larger, the western downs and moors of the southwest had to be negotiated to reach the Atlantic coast.

The region served the ancestors of the modern ports, the Cinque Ports of Sandwich, Dover, Romney, Hythe and Hastings and later Winchelsea and Rye. Each of the former constituent railway companies developed their own ports for the continent; for example, Southampton to Cherbourg and Le Havre, Newhaven to Dieppe, Folkestone to Boulogne and Dover to Calais. The Southern Region continued to operate railway shipping services out of Newhaven, Folkestone and Dover. In addition, ferry services connected from Portsmouth, Southampton and Lymington to the Isle of Wight and from Weymouth to the Channel Islands.

The region also served many holiday resorts including the larger resorts of Margate, Ramsgate, Eastbourne, Brighton, Bognor Regis and Bournemouth, but also many of the remoter resorts such as Allhallows, Sandgate, Ventnor, Lyme Regis, Bude, Padstow and Ilfracombe, all of which no longer have rail services. Associated with the leisure traffic over 20 racecourses were once served by the region. Although the Southern Region developed predominantly as a passenger railway, it also served the Kent coalfield and ran considerable freight services associated with its ports.

The region contained a number of substantial engineering works, including the many crossings of the River Thames, viaducts at Folkestone, Brighton, across the Ouse Valley and at Meldon and 10 tunnels of more than a mile in length. In 1994 the railways of the former region were at last connected to mainland Europe by the Channel Tunnel.

Below left: A Class U 2-6-0 crosses Meldon Viaduct near Okehampton with a ballast train from Meldon Quarry on 7 April 1964. Unlike the nearby quarry, the 120ft high wrought-iron structure is no longer in use, but endures as one of just two great metal railway viaducts remaining in the country. *A. J. Wheeler*

Above: Boundary changes affected the Southern Region, particularly to the west of Salisbury. The southern part of the old Somerset & Dorset Railway, south of Blandford Forum, remained in the Southern Region's area. The first stop north of Blandford was at Shillingstone. Although closed to passengers in 1966 and subsequently allowed to become partly derelict, this station was one of the few to remain on the S&DR when this view was taken in 1995. *Author*

BRITISH RLYS. (Southern Region)

To

ANDOVER TOWN

787/244

London and South Western Ry.

787

FROM WATERLOO TO

COLYFORD

③ Tunnels to the lost Palace

Two great railway men were associated with Crystal Palace. The first was Robert Stephenson who was in charge of the arrangements for the Great Exhibition. It is therefore perhaps not surprising that a forward-looking prefabricated iron-framed and glass building of great uniqueness, designed by Sir Joseph Paxton, was selected to house the Great Exhibition in 1851. The structure, which was dubbed the 'Crystal Palace', was re-erected near Penge in south London after the exhibition closed, and the locality became known as Crystal Palace.

The second famous railway name was that of Isambard Kingdom Brunel who was employed to make the fountains in the Palace gardens work properly. He solved the problem by constructing two water towers which allowed the fountains to soar to a height of 250ft.

The 3¾-mile line from Nunhead to Crystal Palace High Level station was opened in August 1865. At its opening the large twin-vaulted terminal at Crystal Palace High Level was hardly complete and intermediate stations at Honor Oak and Lordship Lane had not been opened. In reaching Crystal Palace the line ran on gradients of up to 1 in 78 and through tunnels under Crescent Wood and Upper Norwood to reach the Palace entrance.

The railway did much to promote the Palace and the substantial station at Crystal Palace High Level was used to capacity on a number of occasions. For the first 30 years the Palace was visited by an average of 2 million people a year. The station was connected directly to the Palace by an ornate and patterned colonnaded subway, built in white and red bricks. An additional station at Upper Sydenham was added to the line in 1884. It is also of note that the French landscape artist Camille Pissarro painted a view of Lordship Lane station on the line in 1871. It is clear from the painting that at that time this area was still quite rural. In 1898 the station was renamed Crystal Palace High Level & Upper Norwood to reflect new residential development in the area. The route was electrified in July 1925 and an intensive service was provided.

Elsewhere along the line ownership of land by Dulwich College prevented development. Furthermore, the established LBSCR route to the Low Level Station at Crystal Palace competed with the SECR line. It also provided direct covered access to the Palace and its existing stations at Sydenham, Forest Hill and Honor Oak Park were relatively close to the SECR stations. Consequently traffic on the route, apart from sporadic heavy use associated with

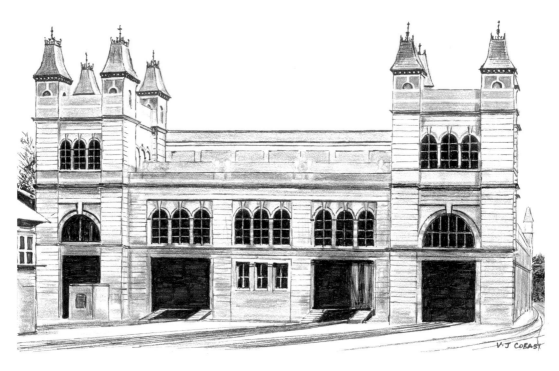

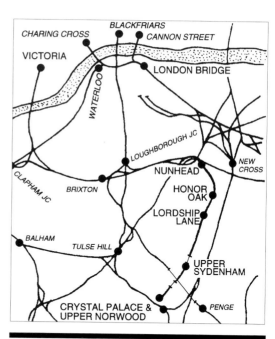

Left: A South Eastern & Chatham Railway poster displaying one of the wide range of events that took place at Crystal Palace. Clearly the railway considered that the Palace had a catchment area covering all of Kent. *Courtesy NRM*

Below left: Crystal Palace High Level station. An original drawing by V. J. Corasi.

Below: An EMU emerges from the Crystal Palace Tunnel to arrive at the High Level station prior to closure in 1954. This was one of the few electrified third rail lines ever to be closed in the London area. *R. C. Riley*

the Palace traffic, was often sparse. The Palace closed for the duration of World War 1. The line was also closed between 1917 and 1919 and for a time at the

end of World War 2 between 1944 and 1946 for economy reasons.

Crystal Palace burnt down in November 1936 and it was acknowledged that rebuilding was unrealistic. With the Palace traffic at an end, the future of the line looked increasingly bleak. The line closed to all traffic in September 1954 and for a time the vast train shed at Crystal Palace remained derelict and unused. After demolition much of the area remained underused for almost three decades before housing development covered a substantial part of the site. A number of other sections of the line have also been built over and there is therefore no possibility of reopening.

Trains still run to Crystal Palace Low Level station. Many traces of the High Level line remain, including the fabulous disused subway that once provided direct access to the Crystal Palace itself. Some sections of the line are also used as footpaths. The Palace is no more, together with the pneumatic and electric tram lines that once ran in the grounds. Yet much of interest has survived, including the bases of Brunel's water towers which endured the fire only to be demolished in 1942.

Above left: The line was heavily engineered and a vast retaining wall ran for a considerable length below Crystal Palace Parade. This view of the redeveloped station site from below the retaining wall was taken in May 1995. *Author*

Above: The entrance to the Crystal Palace Tunnel prior to redevelopment of the station site for housing. For a time part of the site was used for car parking. *P. Hocquard*

Above right: The entrance to the Crystal Palace Tunnel in May 1995. It is interesting that such was the grandeur and weight of a number of the tunnel portals on this line that there has, over the years, been notable settlement of some portals from the main tunnel borelining. *Author*

Right: The subway from Crystal Palace High Level station, under Crystal Palace Parade, to the Palace itself still remains, as this view taken in May 1995 shows. The subway was constructed in 1865 by Italian crypt builders. *Author*

Far right: Map of Crystal Palace in 1938 with the Palace already deleted. *Crown Copyright*

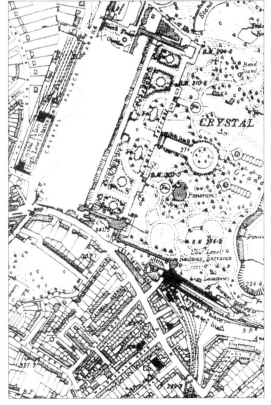

Above: Upper Sydenham station looking towards Crescent Wood Tunnel in the early 1950s. *Ian Allan Library*

Below: Crescent Wood Tunnel in May 1994. Part of the old line from the north entrance of this tunnel to the site of Lordship Lane station is used as a nature trail. *Author*

4 Thames crossings and closures

Blackfriars

Blackfriars takes its name from a Dominican Priory on the site where the friars wore black habits. In modern times a public house, once owned by the London Chatham & Dover Railway (LCDR), takes it name from the friars, together with the station and bridges that cross the tidal reaches of the River Thames here. There are numerous crossings of the Thames and fortunately most remain. An exception in London is at Blackfriars where the original bridge, sometimes known as the Alexandra Bridge, has been partly lost. Designed by Joseph Cubitt, the structure was manufactured at Crumlin in Wales, carried four tracks and had an overall span of 933ft. Opened in December 1864 for the LCDR, it was the first railway crossing of

Left: The 54 famous stones from the old Blackfriars station now on the wall of the present station concourse. *BR*

Below: A view of the run-down Blackfriars station exterior in BR days. Originally called St Pauls and opened in 1886, the station was renamed Blackfriars in 1937. The station remains open, but this frontage was demolished in 1978. *R. J. Marshall*

the Thames into the City of London. This historic structure had its five lattice girder spans demolished in 1985 in favour of the later adjoining bridge that had been opened in 1886. The rationalisation was possible due to the decline of freight using the route.

The many bridges across the Thames are of differing designs, but the LCDR bridge was embellished with huge coats of arms of that railway. In spite

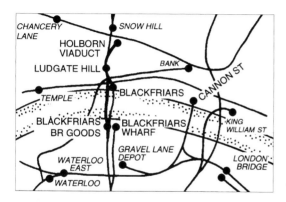

of this, Ruskin complained about this decoration. 'The entire invention of the designer seems to have exhausted itself in exaggerating to an enormous size a weak form of iron nut, and in conveying the information upon it, in large letters, that it belongs to the London Chatham & Dover Railway'. A remaining abutment with its decorative cast-iron capitals has been restored, including the coat of arms of the railway. The bridge's cast-iron columns standing on stone piers still remain in the Thames.

Gravesend

There have been railway closures on the south side of the Thames such as at Battersea and Deptford Wharves and the lines associated with Woolwich Arsenal. At Gravesend substantial disused railway waterside features are still to be found. This riverside town with its Dickensian waterfront was an early pleasure resort. Even before the first railway reached the town, steamers brought thousands of trippers to the area and in particular to Rosherville Gardens, which were located in a sheltered chalk pit. Trips were made along the Thames to the Town Pier which was built in 1834 for Gravesend Corporation.

A scheme to tunnel under the Thames at Gravesend was proposed, but was never proceeded with. However, in 1884 the London Tilbury & Southend Railway was given permission to run passenger ferries and in 1895 purchased the Town Pier. A frequent ferry service soon developed and steam ferries took about 10min to cross this half-mile-wide stretch of the Thames estuary. Connecting trains to London from Tilbury station were able to compete on journey times with those from Gravesend.

Gravesend developed as an industrial area and as a port for overseas liners. Consequently the London

Far left: The decorative cast-iron crest of the former London Chatham & Dover Railway bridge over the Thames at Blackfriars. Clearly the links with Kent, Victoria and its opening date of 1864 are apparent from this remaining feature of the lost bridge. I will leave the reader to judge Ruskin's criticisms of the design. *Author*

Left: The Blackfriar public house was once railway-owned. The building is listed as being of architectural importance and the 1905 interior décor of the friars, by Henry Pool, is a good excuse for a visit. *Author*

Bottom left: Although the upper decking of this bridge at Blackfriars has been removed, the cast-iron pillars remain in the Thames. They were built on stones from the old Westminster road bridge which was demolished in 1861. Although redevelopment at either end has precluded any future railway reuse of the partly dismantled bridge, there have been plans to put an innovative building over the Thames using the old bridge supports. *Author*

Below: A Wainwright Class C 0-6-0, No 1876, heads a Rotterdam boat train at Gravesend West Street on 11 June 1938. *H. C. Casserley*

Gravesend was provided with three levels to allow for the considerable tidal range of this part of the Thames and at high tide 40ft of water was available at the pier head. Although the station was a terminus, it was built in a junction arrangement, with one platform heading towards the pier and the other heading towards the town. Boat trains did not start using the line until 1916 and the Batavier Line ran connecting services to Rotterdam. Intermediate stations were provided at Southfleet and Rosherville, whilst a halt was opened at Longfield in 1913.

The terminus at Gravesend became known as Gravesend West Street in 1899 and Gravesend West in 1949. The line was never electrified and the inevitable decline set in. Rosherville Gardens, which closed as far back as 1910, had fallen into decay and the adjoining station became an unstaffed halt from 1928. European sailings were switched to Tilbury after World War 2. The shorter rail route to London via Dartford and even the ferry route via Tilbury all competed with the branch. As a consequence the line provided for mainly local traffic and closed to passengers in August 1953. The line was singled in 1959 and freight continued to the paper mills and riverside at Gravesend until March 1968.

Although the pier at Gravesend West remains almost as originally constructed, the bulk of the station buildings, which it has to be said were not particularly attractive, have been demolished. The pier is in a deteriorating condition and there are frost cracks to some of the supports, although the Thames last froze across here in 1895! The tunnel that led to the station area has been deepened and converted into a road. It is still possible to reach Gravesend by train and cross the Thames nearby by ferry, but the connecting rail services at Tilbury ended in the 1960s, whilst the passenger station at Tilbury Riverside closed in November 1992. As to the future, part of the old Gravesend West line may be used as a connection to the new Channel Tunnel rail link, fulfilling once again its original purpose as a route to the continent.

Chatham & Dover Railway decided to compete with the existing services to Gravesend, building a five-mile branch from a junction near Longfield. The line ran in a relatively straight northeasterly direction, crossing the Dartford to Gravesend line to reach a new Thames pier at Gravesend. The branch was opened in April 1886 and a ceremonial river crossing was made to Tilbury Docks which opened on the same date.

The line involved extensive earthworks and was seen as a potential future main route. The new pier at

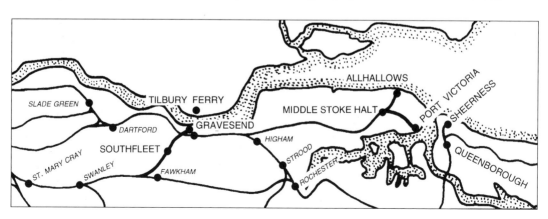

Left: The abandoned Gravesend West (Street was deleted from the name in 1949) station entrance to the pier from street level, seen here in 1989. Much of the station area has subsequently been given over to retail uses. *Author*

Above: A covered way ran from the station to the pier head; this remained intact when this view was taken in April 1995. The closed Tilbury Riverside station can just be seen on the other side of the Thames. *Author*

Centre right: A view of the pier looking east, towards the sea, in May 1995 and showing the considerable tidal range on this part of the Thames estuary. *Author*

Right: The derelict, but listed, Town Pier at Gravesend, where connections could once be made for trains at Tilbury Riverside station, photographed here during a spring tide in April 1995. A ferry service still operates across the Thames at Gravesend, but not from this pier. *Author*

Allhallows-on-Sea was not located entirely on Thames mud, but on a short stretch of mixed shingle, quite unique on this part of the Thames estuary. It was also in some respects the nearest holiday resort on the coast for many in southeast London. Indeed in its first year of opening the route attracted much traffic, but it never became a major resort and the line closed to all traffic in December 1961.

Port Victoria

The line from Hoo Junction ran some 11 miles to Port Victoria, where a ferry once crossed the mouth of the River Medway to connect to Queenborough and where in turn ships once ran to Holland. However, this route could not compete with the direct line to Queenborough and in 1901 the ferry service was withdrawn and in 1916 Port Victoria Pier itself was closed. Passenger services continued to Port Victoria until June 1951, but freight to the Isle of Grain oil terminal still uses the branch.

It was from the Port Victoria line that the Southern Railway in 1932 constructed an eventually double-track line from Stoke Junction some 1¾ miles across the flat Allhallows marshland to the remote coastal settlement of Allhallows-on-Sea. Although since closed, this new line was not such an unsound idea.

Top: A Kirtley Class R 0-4-4T No 31662 takes water at Allhallows-on-Sea in September 1952. *P. Ransome-Wallis*

Above: A BRCW Type 3 (Class 33) and two unusually ancient non-corridor carriages for diesel haulage, await departure from Allhallows-on-Sea shortly before closure of the line. *D. Lawrence*

Left: A Wainwright 0-4-4T, No A311, in Southern livery at Port Victoria on 26 March 1930. The pier has now long since been lost in the midst of an industrial complex in the area. *H. C. Casserley*

5 A Canterbury tale

In medieval times pilgrims to Canterbury were regaled with Chaucer's colourful tales. A later tale of equal interest relates to the city's first railway. Although the industrial revolution did not influence southern England to the same extent as the north, Canterbury was one of the most substantial towns in southern England and direct communications to the coast, other than by the continually silting up River Stour, were required. At first a canal was considered, but eventually a railway was decided upon. George Stephenson was the engineer and the Canterbury & Whitstable Railway, running six miles from Canterbury to the coast, was opened in May 1830.

Being such an early route, the line was unique in many ways and at first stationary winding engines were required on the steepest sections. Travelling north to the coast from Canterbury, the route was forced to cut under high land at Tyler Hill by means of a 1,012yd tunnel, the first ever to be used by passenger trains. The tunnel was of a particularly narrow bore and on a rising gradient of 1 in 56 towards Whitstable. As a consequence in later years specially cut-down chimneys and domes were provided for engines using the line. Equally, locomotives worked up through the tunnel cab-first to the considerable advantage of the footplate crew. Beyond Tyler Hill,

where a halt was provided, the line continued to run almost due north and under a substantial bridge that was later constructed over the line for the A299 Thanet Way. Finally, the branch crossed over the main North Kent coast line to reach Whitstable and its railway-built harbour.

The isolated section of line was never particularly financially successful and an early rationalisation diverted trains from the original terminal in Canterbury to the nearby Canterbury West station in 1846. Consideration was also given to making rail connections to the North Kent line at Whitstable. Costs precluded this, but a halt was opened in 1916 and provided foot connection to the main line station. The line closed to passenger services at the beginning of 1931, but it remained in use for freight to

Below: A Class R1 0-6-0T, No 31010, with a short chimney, reduced boiler mountings and cut-down cab, running around brake vans at Whitstable Harbour station on 29 November 1952, the last day of services. Note the decorations. The line was reopened for some days during the following February when the main line to Whitstable was closed by severe flooding.
P. Ransome-Wallis

Whitstable Harbour until December 1952. However, this was not quite to be the end of the line, for it reopened briefly for three days in February 1953 when the east coast floods damaged the main North Kent coast line.

Fortunately one of the original locomotives used on part of the line, *Invicta*, remains. This 12hp 0-4-0 was built at Robert Stephenson's works in Newcastle and the resemblance to Stephenson's *Rocket* is striking. After many years of being displayed in the open, the locomotive is now preserved at the Canterbury Heritage Museum.

The line remains unobstructed for much of its route, with the exception of Tyler Hill Tunnel which suffered a roof collapse in 1974. Sections of the old route are used as footpaths and consideration is being given to reopening the route as a tram line —but that is a future Canterbury tale.

Above: The original Whitstable Harbour station with the bare basics of facilities. A later station built by the South Eastern Railway in 1894 obviated the need for all passenger trains to cross the nearby coast road. *Ian Allan Library*

Right: In comparison to the small scale of the original bridges on the route, the bridge built for the Thanet Way in 1935, to carry the then new A299 road over the railway, was a massive concrete structure. The bridge and roadside abutments, which are shown in this view, remain and are shown here in May 1995. *Author*

Above: One of the oldest railway overbridges in the world and viewed here close to Whitstable main line station. The bridge, dating from 1830, was demolished in 1969, an act that is recorded locally as one of official vandalism; the iron railings to the road remain. *LPC*

Centre right: An adjacent second bridge was built in 1861 for the North Kent line to pass underneath the Canterbury and Whitstable branch. The abutment of the bridge can be seen in this view, together with the platforms of Whitstable station. A pedestrian connection was made in 1916 between the main line station and a halt on the branch, which was situated close to the overbridge abutment. Note the iron railings remain in 1995. *Author*

Right: On the northern outskirts of Canterbury the remains of an original underbridge can still be seen, as this view taken in May 1995 shows. *Author*

NEAR HERE WAS THE TERMINUS
OF THE
CANTERBURY AND WHITSTABLE
RAILWAY, 1830
(GEORGE STEPHENSON, ENGINEER)
THE WORLD'S FIRST RAILWAY
SEASON TICKETS ISSUED HERE 1834

Above: This plaque has been mounted on Canterbury West station. It records the fact that the first season tickets were issued on the C&WR in 1834. *Author*

Below: The original C&WR terminus at Canterbury involved the branch crossing the main Margate to Ashford line on the level to the right of the signalbox. In 1995, when this view was taken, the box still straddled the tracks. In 1846 all passenger trains were diverted to the then new and still-remaining Canterbury West station. *Author*

Hoppers to Hawkhurst

The groups of oast houses that once used to dry hops before dispatch to the brewing centres are a reminder of the golden days of traditional hopping in Kent. Before mechanisation, vast crowds of Londoners descended on the 'Garden of England' for the hop-picking season which was in the late summer. The railways ran 'hoppers' specials and these trains provided a fillip for some of the Kent branch lines with access to hop gardens.

One such line was the 11½-mile ex-SECR route from Paddock Wood to Hawkhurst. The line opened as far as Goudhurst in October 1892 and was completed, via a short tunnel, to Hawkhurst by September of the following year. Running in a generally southerly direction from Paddock Wood the steeply graded and curved line ran through remote and relatively precipitous hills that form the High Weald. The steeply undulating hills caused other problems. The station at Horsmonden was reasonably well sited, but others could have hardly been more inconvenient. The station for Goudhurst was sited at the very foot of the long hill leading to the settlement, the station at Cranbrook was located almost two miles from the main centre and at Hawkhurst the station was sited on high land to the north of the town. However, the Kent & East Sussex Railway called one of its stations 'Junction Road for Hawkhurst' even though it was about three miles from Hawkhurst.

The line was a real backwater and in later years, although good connections were provided with main line trains at Paddock Wood, only a limited weekday service was run and there were few regular commuters. For many years the line survived on the rich agricultural traffic and more than a million pot plants were transported from Hawkhurst station in some years. There were also of course the 'hoppers' specials-passenger trains that ran to stations on the line.

The branch's decline, was due not only to the growth in road transport, but also to a number of other factors. These included the fact that Hawkhurst was never really intended as the final terminus and provided insufficient traffic, but plans to extend the line, including a link between Cranbrook and Tenterden St Michaels, were never realised.

Below: Goudhurst station with Class C 0-6-0 No 31717 and Class D 4-4-0 No 31729, double-heading a hop-pickers' return special from Hawkhurst to London Bridge on 29 September 1951. A considerable number of hop-pickers and their luggage await the train. *K. G. Carr*

Above: Life without the train in deepest Kent on
1 April 1995. Horses and coach cross bridge No 1468,
so designated under a Kent County Council bridge
numbering scheme, over the Hawkhurst branch near
Goudhurst.
Author

Below: The overgrown single trackbed of the Hawkhurst
branch near Goudhurst on 1 April 1995.
Author

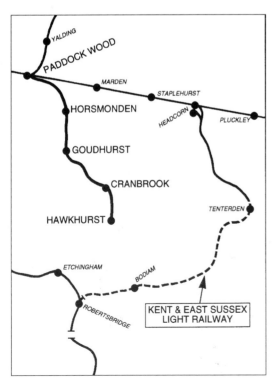

The inconvenient location of many of the stations from the settlements they were supposed to serve and the need to change trains at the main line stifled the growth of commuting to London. Finally, the hop-picking season, although only adding a temporary fillip to the line's revenue, became mechanised and the 'hoppers specials', plus the associated freight, disappeared.

The line was never considered for electrification or modernisation and closed in June 1961. Today many traces remain, including a number of bridges and the tunnel. Part of the station yard at Horsmonden is used as a garage, that at Goudhurst has been demolished, but Cranbrook remains in residential use and the station site at Hawkhurst is in commercial use, retaining most of its brick buildings and the original signalbox.

Left: An ex-SECR up home signal at Cranbrook, viewed on 27 May 1961.
J. Scrace

Below: The 5pm push-pull train leaving Cranbrook propelled by Class H 0-4-4T No 31517 in September 1959.
H. P. White

Opposite above: The main Cranbrook station buildings remained, when this view was taken in April 1995, although in a modified form. *Author*

Opposite below: Class H 0-4-4T No 31543 pauses at Hawkhurst after working the 12.30pm from Paddock Wood and before returning with the 1.5pm on 27 May 1961. Closure came the following month. *J. Scrace*

Above: Hawkhurst station in April 1995. Many of the brick structures remain here and along the course of the line, although the more lightly-built corrugated-iron buildings have largely disappeared. *Author*

Below left: Hawkhurst signalbox has been saved and restored, as this view taken in April 1995 shows. *Author*

Below right: A view of the restored Hawkhurst signalbox taken on 1 April 1995. *Author*

7 *Au revoir* Dover Marine

There are occasions when the closure of a line or station seems unjustified, unreasonable and short-sighted. Equally, there have been occasions when progress and development of the railway system have rendered existing lines and stations superfluous.

The first impression on arrival in any country is often influenced by the quality of its public transport. Dover had for many years been the gateway from the continent, but at the turn of the century many complaints were made about the facilities provided. Consequently a scheme to reclaim 11¾ acres from the sea on the east side of Admiralty Pier, to provide a station larger than Charing Cross, was prepared. The new station building covered an area of about three acres. It consisted of two huge island platforms 700ft long and 63ft wide, protected by an overall roof some 800ft long. This was a bold scheme that on completion must have truly impressed those arriving at Dover. Although Dover Marine station was first used by the public in January 1919, when services again resumed to the continent after World War 1, it had in fact been opened in January 1915 and been used for some time as an ambulance station.

So magnificent was the station that the South Eastern & Chatham Railway's war memorial is located here, rather than in London as was the case with many other railways. Unveiled in October 1922 the memorial has 556 names from World War 1, followed by 626 names from World War 2. The massive bronze group was designed by the sculptor W. C. H. King. Such is the weight of this structure that when originally constructed, steps led to the solid stone base of the sculpture. Today these have disappeared as the memorial sinks slowly into the reclaimed land on which the station was built.

The station was designed principally to provide convenient access to ships for the continent, but a substantial covered passage also ran from the station to the nearby town and to what was originally called the Lord Warden Hotel. This mainly four-storey building was designed by Samuel Beazley for the SER and opened in 1853. The hotel, which closed in September 1939, was later converted to offices by the Southern Railway and sold in 1946. The building remains and is called Southern House.

Below left: The ultimate in 1950s luxury to Dover as 'Britannia' class No 70004 *William Shakespeare* heads the 'Golden Arrow' train near Sandling Junction in 1952.
A. C. Cawston

Right: On arrival and departure at Dover Marine in the 1950s many porters were available. Indeed there appear almost as many railway staff as passengers on the platform.
A. Hasenson

Below right: The imposing, but increasingly desolate, Dover Marine station on 24 September 1994. *Author*

Below: The war memorial at Dover Marine was unveiled in October 1922 and contains 556 names from World War 1 and 626 names from World War 2. The bronze group was designed by W. C. H. King.
Author

In 1980 Dover Marine station was renamed as Dover Western Docks, but with the increasing passenger use of the Channel Tunnel services, maritime stations were closed in France, together with Dover Western Docks station which closed to passengers in September 1994. The station's last day was marked by over 400 enthusiasts who arrived aboard a special steam train to say *au revoir* to the station. Empty EMU stock was temporarily stabled in the station until March 1995. There are no plans to demolish the structure which has been put to new uses in a redevelopment of the area.

DOVER FOR THE CONTINENT

← **THEN**
ONE SAILING A WEEK

NOW
↓ SEVEN SAILINGS A DAY

1850

FROM DOVER

dep.			
10.00 for Boulogne	—	Motorists and Cars.	
12.20 „ Dunkerque	—	„ „ „	
12.20 „ Ostend	—	from Victoria 10.00	
13.00 „ Calais	—	„ „ { 10.30	
		„ { 11.00 "Golden Arrow"	
13.30 „ Ostend	—	Motorists and Cars.	
16.50 „ Ostend	—	from Victoria 14.30	
0.40 „ Dunkerque	—	„ „ 22.00 "Night Ferry"	

Summer Service — until October 7th, 1950

BRITISH RAILWAYS

1950

100 YEARS OF SERVICE BY THE SHORT SEA ROUTE

Above: British Railways promoted Dover as 'The Short Sea Route'. This 'then and now' poster of 1950 shows development of the route, but now itself looks decidedly dated in the context of cross-Channel traffic growth and the Channel Tunnel.
Courtesy NRM

Left: One of the deserted waiting areas in the vast station, viewed here in September 1994 and having a decidedly continental look about it.
Author

Right: Dover harbour in 1908 *(top)* and in 1937 *(below)*.
Crown Copyright

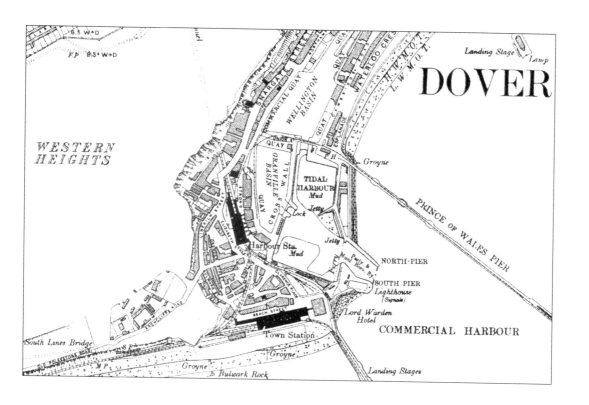

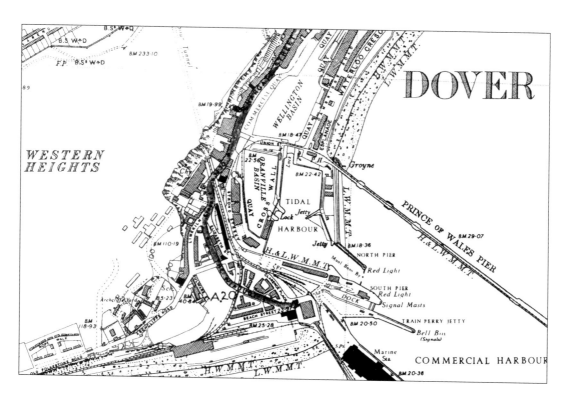

Above: The landward approach to the station viewed here in September 1994. The entrance was conveniently located almost opposite one of the entrances to the former Lord Warden Hotel, which can be seen just to the right of this view. *Author*

Left: A series of passageways connected to and from the station and a substantial one ran towards the town, but there were few passengers when this view was taken in September 1994. *Author*

Below: The Italianate-influenced and listed Southern House, originally the SER's Lord Warden Hotel. Opened in 1853, guests have included Charles Dickens, Napoleon III, Queen Victoria and Prince Albert. The hotel closed in 1939 with the outbreak of World War 2 and was subsequently turned into offices. *Author*

⑧ West from the Wells

The development of Tunbridge Wells was due very much to its iron-rich spa water. A legacy of visits by Queen Victoria enabled 'Royal' to be added to its name in 1909, by which time the town was well served by railways. The line from Tunbridge Wells to Groombridge, East Grinstead and on to Three Bridges was opened in sections. The first section was a single line from Three Bridges to East Grinstead, opened in July 1855. The line was extended to Groombridge and Tunbridge Wells, opening throughout, again as a single line, by October 1866.

The complete London Brighton & South Coast Railway's (LBSCR) 20¼-mile link competed, for a time, for London to Tunbridge Wells traffic with the South Eastern & Chatham Railway and although a slightly longer route, was marketed by the LBSCR as 'the pleasant route'. For many years this useful cross-country line was well used and spurs were provided to Lewes and the Cuckoo line at Groombridge and to the Bluebell line at East Grinstead. Services were developed in Southern Railway days and the Tunbridge Wells (West was added to the name by the Southern)-Groombridge section became a particularly busy single-track line.

Although well used, it is said by some that because the route was not duplicated by a first class main road

it was not electrified by the Southern. The first closure was the remote High Rocks Halt in May 1952. However, there was arguably some degree of duplication with the Tonbridge-Redhill line and subsequently the route was proposed for closure in the Beeching Report. The 17-mile section from Ashurst Junction, near Groombridge, via East Grinstead High Level to Three Bridges closed in January 1967. The last service ran with a silver band on board playing Auld Lang Syne. It left East Grinstead to the roar of fireworks and fog detonators, a porter laid a wreath on the track and over 100 spectators paid their last respects.

At this time it was generally considered that the remaining section of route from Groombridge to Tunbridge Wells West was secure. Indeed, far from closure, it was considered that the line from Uckfield through Isfield to Lewes should be reopened. It therefore came as a bombshell when it was announced that the Tunbridge Wells West to Groombridge section, a

Below: A Fairburn 2-6-4T, No 42088, awaits departure from Tunbridge Wells West with the 11.7am to Victoria on 13 September 1958. *A. W. Martin*

useful long-term future link, would be closed in July 1985.

After closure the substantial station buildings at Tunbridge Wells West remained in a neglected state and there was concern for the future of this attractive listed building. However, the structure was saved and turned into a restaurant in association with a supermarket development of the station area. The Tunbridge Wells West to Groombridge section has been preserved as the Spa Valley Railway. The intention is also to keep the route at Tunbridge Wells West free from development so that in future the opportunity will still exist for through running from Brighton to Tunbridge Wells.

My diary records a trip on the route:

1 May 1965: Took a train from Reading South to Redhill, which was slightly boring. Then I grabbed a train from Redhill to Three Bridges. Here I saw a 'Brighton Belle' pass through the station with great sparks coming from the conductor rails. The trip from Three Bridges to Tunbridge Wells West was very beautiful. The station names have a Welsh ring and long stops were made at them. A party of weird people were on the station at Tunbridge Wells West, waiting for the train to Eastbourne.

Apart from the preserved section between Tunbridge Wells West and Groombridge, a section of

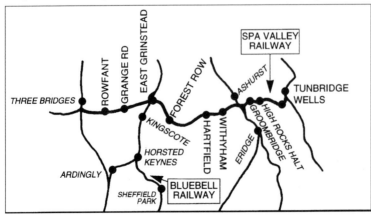

the line at East Grinstead has been converted into a road. The bulk of the remaining route has been turned into a footpath. Between East Grinstead and Three Bridges it is known as the Worth Way, while the section from East Grinstead towards Groombridge is known as the Forest Way. Furthermore, the related route south from East Grinstead to Sheffield Park is preserved as part of the Bluebell Railway

Above left: Approaching Tunbridge Wells West on 6 May 1980 is a Class 207 DEMU No 1306 with the 16.15 Tonbridge to Eridge service. *Brian Morrison*

Above: Back to back, BR Standard Class 4 tanks Nos 80144 and 80065 at Tunbridge Wells West on the 1.9pm from Victoria on 4 August 1962. *L. Sandler*

Right: A view taken in July 1989, after closure of Tunbridge Wells West station in July 1985. *Author*

Below right: The deteriorating state of Tunbridge Wells West station in July 1989. The site is now a supermarket, but the main station building, with its attractive clock tower, is currently in use as a restaurant. *Author*

Above: BR Standard Class 4 2-6-4T No 80152 on a Tunbridge Wells West to Victoria train at East Grinstead on 20 August 1960. Note the bubble car behind the signal. *G. Kitchenside*

Left: The line west of Tunbridge Wells West passed by High Rocks where a halt was once provided. This view, which was taken in July 1989, was prior to the reopening of the route as the preserved Spa Valley Railway. *Author*

Below left: East Grinstead High Level station looking west. Lines to the left were to Three Bridges, those to the right joined up with the Oxted and London line. The platform from which the photograph was taken was used by the Three Bridges trains; the other platform by the Oxted to Tunbridge Wells West trains. Today the High Level station has gone and the entire remaining station area has been remodelled. *P. Ransome-Wallis*

and at Isfield a 1½-mile length of track on the former Lewes to Tunbridge Wells route has been preserved.

Right: The remains of Rowfant station in May 1995. Much of the route of the old line is now used as a public footpath. *Author*

Below centre: BR Standard Class 4 2-6-4T No 80019 stands at Rowfant with the 18.07 Three Bridges to East Grinstead train on 11 June 1965, the last day of steam services over the line. *G. D. King*

Bottom right: DEMU No 1316 pauses with the 13.08 Three Bridges to Tunbridge Wells West train at Grange Road on 28 November 1964. *J. Scrace*

⑨ Death of the Cuckoo

The line from Polegate, near Eastbourne, to Redgate Mill Junction, south of Eridge on the Tunbridge Wells to Lewes line, was an extension of a branch that was opened from Polegate to Hailsham in May 1849. Hailsham is a substantial market town which in earlier days was even more important than Eastbourne. The first plans were for a narrow gauge railway northwards to Tunbridge Wells, but eventually a standard gauge single line opened between Hailsham and Heathfield in April 1880 and was extended to Eridge in September of that year. In addition the track was diverted at Polegate to ensure through running to Eastbourne rather than Lewes.

The 20½ miles of the complete route from Eridge travelled through attractive countryside on its route towards Polegate, running through part of the Weald before entering a 200yd tunnel under the centre of Heathfield. Continuing south to Hailsham, again the railway served the centre of the town. At Hellingly, a 500V dc electric tramway ran, until March 1959, to the nearby and huge Hellingly Hospital. Finally, on the Pevensey Levels, the route reached Polegate on the Lewes to Eastbourne line. The line had many typical features of the LBSCR, including the attractive station buildings. These originally had mock Queen Anne timber and plaster upper floors, but because of water seepage were later hung with their equally distinctive tiles.

The Weald has seen some interesting birds such as the precariously surviving Dartford Warbler, but the route became known as the Cuckoo line because of the Cuckoo Fair at Hailsham. Although the line remained single and was not electrified, there was considerable traffic and many stations were well located in relation to the settlements they served. However, the timetable was revised in 1964 which made services and connections more inconvenient and, partly as a result of this, the following year closure was announced. A fight was launched against closure, but the main section of the route, from Eridge to Hailsham, closed to passengers in June 1965. The last train carried the words 'Farewell faithful servant'. Freight ran from Polegate as far as Heathfield until April 1968. The surviving passenger stump, with its level crossings and inconvenient routeing to London, was hardly likely to be viable and the remaining section of line from Hailsham to Polegate closed in September 1968.

Part of the line has been turned into a road at Mayfield, but south of Heathfield a 10-mile section to Polegate has been converted into the award-winning Cuckoo Trail for cyclists, walkers and horseriders. Indeed, at busy times this route appears to have more users now than at any time previously. Sculptured

Below: 'Farewell faithful servant' were the words on the last train. Flowers adorn the front of BR Standard Class 4 2-6-4T No 80142 as it leaves Mayfield with the 09.25 Eastbourne to Tunbridge Wells West service on 11 June 1965, the last day of passenger services. *J. Scrace*

mileposts replace the originals; each has a cuckoo hidden within! Many of the structures associated with the line also remain including the station buildings at Rotherfield, Mayfield, Heathfield and Hellingly; the last retaining its platform canopy.

Above: Mayfield station in April 1995. The main buildings remain, but a road has replaced the railway. *Author*

Below: BR Standard Class 4 2-6-4T No 80034 at Heathfield with the 13.40 to Eastbourne on 24 May 1965. Argos Hill Tunnel and the main station buildings can be seen in the background. *J. Scrace*

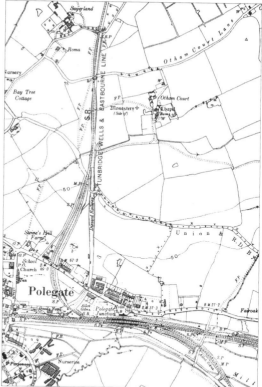

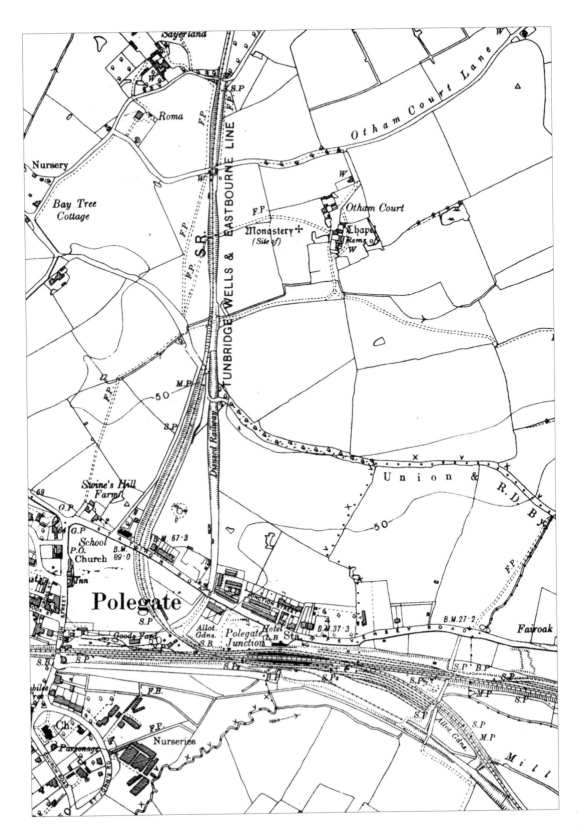

44

Left: The first 1849 disused, and later 1881, link to Polegate station in 1928. *Crown Copyright*

Above: The imposing Heathfield station house buildings seen here in May 1995. A local supply of natural gas lit the station between 1898 and 1934. *Author*

Right: The southern portal of Argos Hill Tunnel in April 1995. *Author*

Below: BR Standard Class 4 2-6-4 No 80072 stands at Horam station on Friday 28 May 1965 with the 15.14 Tunbridge Wells West to Eastbourne train. The station name had been simplified to Horam from the original Waldron and Horeham Road. *S. Tallis*

Above: A distinctive Southern concrete nameboard and lamp post remain at Horam as part of the Cuckoo Trail in April 1995. Unfortunately none of the other buildings associated with the station remain. *Author*

Left: Hellingly station looking north and showing the overhead electrified spur to the nearby hospital on the right of this view. A wooden platform once provided interchange for the hospital with the main line, until passenger services ended in 1931. The spur closed to goods in 1959.
Ian Allan Library

Left: Hellingly station buildings remained remarkably unchanged when this view, looking south, was taken in April 1995. *Author*

Above: DEMU No 1119 on the 15.49 to Eastbourne, at Hailsham on 5 September 1968.
J. Scrace

Below: Although the station buildings at Hailsham have been demolished, the bridge to the north of the station and route of the line remain in use as the Cuckoo Trail, as this view taken in April 1995 shows. *Author*

10 A Belle to a Brighton byway

The Prince Regent travelled to Brighton in 1783 and so began the development of this popular seaside resort. The London to Brighton line was opened in 1841 and this soon hastened the town's growth. A trip down the line to Brighton is always a pleasure, but was even more so on the 'Brighton Belle'. My diary records a particularly interesting trip on this train when the second class supplement was 20p:

28 April 1972: Went down to Brighton on the 'Brighton Belle'. Two old dears were in the seats opposite (I was much younger then). When the steward came round they asked what was available. When told of the food and drink they asked for brandies and salmon sandwiches which seemed a little extravagant. When asked to pay for these, events turned nasty. They were having none of it. 'Fetch the head waiter' they screamed. Along came the ticket collector. 'This four shilling ticket entitles us to as much food and drink as we want does it not?'

Below: The Kemp Town terminus with a LBSCR Tank shown here in about 1900. Although only one main platform was provided, the design of the station was such to enable considerable potential for further expansion. *LPC*

The answer was of course no! Sadly, the 'Brighton Belle' made its final run a few days later.

On arrival at Brighton there is much of railway interest in the town including the still operational Volk's Electric Railway, the first public electric line in the country which opened in 1883. There was also once an urban branch line in the town. The 1½-mile route from Kemp Town Junction near London Road station, on the Brighton to Lewes line, to the terminus at Kemp Town opened in August 1869. It was a particularly heavily engineered route and included a four-teen-arched viaduct and a 1,024yd tunnel. A substantial terminus area, in anticipation of increasing traffic, was provided at Kemp Town.

Although close to the sea, Kemp Town did not develop a significant holiday trade and most traffic on the line was of a local suburban nature. The branch involved a change of trains at Brighton, where for many years a service was provided on a regular half hour frequency. Two halts were opened at Lewes Road and betwen 1906 and 1911 at Hartington Road, but the line could not compete with more direct trams. With main line electrification to Brighton, the branch was not included in electrification schemes and was an early casualty, closing for passengers in January 1933.

The line continued for freight until June 1971 and a number of enthusiasts' specials were operated over the branch before closure. Since closure the viaduct

on the route has been demolished and the cuttings filled. The dilapidated terminal was also demolished and the extensive site is now an industrial area. Today very little trace of the branch remains.

Right: A Southern Region poster showing the daily timings of the all Pullman 'Brighton Belle'. Even later attempts at harmonisation of the sets into standard BR blue and grey livery failed to dim the attraction of these Pullman units.
Courtesy NRM

Below: Class 08 0-6-0 No D3669 shunts at Kemp Town station on 3 April 1969.
J. M. Tolson

THE
BRIGHTON BELLE
ALL-PULLMAN TRAIN

DAILY THROUGHOUT THE YEAR			
WEEKDAYS			
LONDON (VICTORIA) dep	11 0 am	3 0 pm	7 0 pm
BRIGHTON . . arr	12 noon	4 0 pm	8 0 pm
BRIGHTON . . dep	1 25 pm	5 25 pm	8 25 pm
LONDON (VICTORIA) arr	2 25 pm	6 25 pm	9 25 pm
SUNDAYS			
LONDON (VICTORIA) dep	11 0 am	7 0 pm	
BRIGHTON . . arr	12 noon	8 0 pm	
BRIGHTON . . dep	5 25 pm	8 25 pm	
LONDON (VICTORIA) arr	6 25 pm	9 25 pm	

FOR FURTHER INFORMATION PLEASE ENQUIRE AT STATIONS AND TRAVEL AGENTS

(SOUTHERN)

Top left: The decaying station buildings at Kemp Town in August 1969, 100 years after opening. The van was used as an office and mess room.
J. Vaughan

Bottom left: The decaying exterior of Kemp Town station on 3 March 1969. The station has subsequently been demolished, but the nearby London Road station on the Brighton to Lewes line remains and is of a very similar design.
J. M. Tolson

Top right: A narrow-bodied Hastings unit waits to depart at 17.30 from Kemp Town to Brighton on 26 June 1971, one of several specials for enthusiasts over the branch.
C. S. Heaps

Right: Overgrown tracks at Kemp Town station on 29 June 1971, just after all services had ended. *M. Baker*

Below: Track layout at Kemp Town station.
Crown Copyright

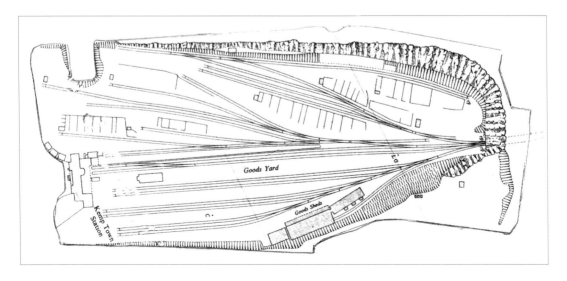

Right: The imposing southern portal to the 1,024yd-long Kemp Town Tunnel in LBSCR days. Note the signalbox bell.
LPC

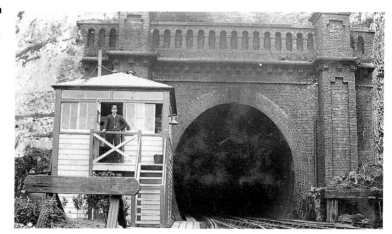

Centre: The same Kemp Town Tunnel entrance in May 1995. The station area is now an industrial estate and this portal is one of the few surviving features of the branch.
Author

Below: The truncated Kemp Town branch viaduct over the Lewes Road in Brighton in 1981. Completed in 1869, the largest arch was over the Lewes Road. Balustrades on the parapet gave the structure a distinctive appearance and, although listed, by 1995 all trace of the viaduct had long since disappeared.
B. K. Cooper

No. **161082**
BRITISH RAILWAYS BOARD
PULLMAN SERVICES
PASSENGER'S CHECK   Good for this Trip only when accompanied by an appropriate Railway Ticket.

PASSENGERS ARE EARNESTLY REQUESTED TO SEE THAT TICKETS ARE TORN FROM A BOOK, SIGNED AND DATED AND TO DESTROY THE TICKET AT THE END OF THE JOURNEY.

BRIGHTON BELLE One Seat
From BRIGHTON to VICTORIA
20p   Date ....
.... CHIEF STEWARD
28 APR 1972
SEE CONDITIONS AT BACK

The boarding school known as Christ's Hospital has since 1902 been located near Horsham. It has been served, from April of that year, by the nearby Christ's Hospital station, which was built on an imposing scale to reflect the school. Located on the Horsham to Bognor Regis line, at one time two former London Brighton & South Coast Railway secondary routes connected with the main line here. One line ran north from the station, which was originally called Stammerham Junction, to Peasmarsh Junction south of Guildford. A second line ran south from Itchingfield Junction to Horsham Line Junction, just west of Shoreham-by-Sea.

The northern route to Guildford opened, after some difficulties, in October 1865. Although built as a single-line branch, with steep gradients and weight-restricted bridges, the 15½-mile link embraced considerable earthworks, including a 381yd tunnel at Baynards. It used a similar route to that of the Wey and Arun Canal near Guildford. Cranleigh, which claims to be England's largest village, with over 10,000 dwellings, together with Bramley provided most of the passenger traffic. Fuller's earth and bricks however were dispatched from Baynards. All these stations provided crossing points, but traffic was essentially of a local nature.

The line was never electrified and the absence of through trains to London reduced its commuting potential. It also ran through a relatively remote area. It was therefore no real surprise when it was identified in the Beeching Report for services to be withdrawn and was closed in June 1965. Three extra coaches were added to the last train to accommodate all those who wished to say farewell, whilst many pupils from the Christ's Hospital school gathered to see the last service.

After closure a society was established to preserve the route, but the decision was eventually taken for much of the line to be turned into a footpath, although reopening as a railway is still a possibility. Cranleigh station is now an industrial estate, Baynards remains almost unchanged since closure, Rudgwick has flats on the old station yard and Slinfold caravans, yet it is still possible to walk past the old station sites. At Christ's Hospital, the once substantial junction with its many platforms and buildings, has been reduced to a bare minimum, but remains open.

A second 17-mile link from a junction about ½ mile south of Christ's Hospital followed the River Adur and its estuary, which cuts through the South Downs, to the coast at Shoreham-by-Sea. This link, which was opened in September 1861 and doubled by 1879, did not provide the through traffic anticipated, as it was duplicated to some extent by the Brighton and the Mid-Sussex lines. The line did provide a useful diversionary route and at one time electrification was considered. Steam was replaced by DEMUs in 1964, but in spite of this the line closed in March 1966, except for the southern section from Shoreham to the Beeding Cement Works for freight, although this traffic ceased by March 1988.

Much of this line has also been turned into a footpath. At West Grinstead part of the station complex remains and even an old station lamp can be seen in a nearby front garden. At Steyning and Bramber the

Left: The imposing entrance to Christ's Hospital station. Opened in 1902 and built on an imposing scale, not unlike the nearby Christ's Hospital school, the station remains open, but traffic has never met expectations and the building in this view was demolished in 1972. *J. Scrace*

Top: BRCW Type 3 No D6572 leaves Christ's Hospital with the 16.36 Horsham to Guildford train on 27 March 1965.
J. Scrace

Above: With the exception of the signalbox, subway and some platforms, Christ's Hospital station was demolished and rationalised after closure of the branches, as this view of demolition in progress on 15 October 1972 shows.
J. Scrace

Below left: One of the platforms that once provided for the Guildford branch at Christ's Hospital seen in May 1995, very considerably overgrown. Though the buildings have been demolished, the signalbox and signal remained *in situ* in 1995.
J. Scrace

Right: An ex-LBSCR Class C2X 0-6-0 heads a freight train through Rudgwick *en route* to Christ's Hospital on an unidentified summer's day, but probably in the 1950s.
Ian Allan Library

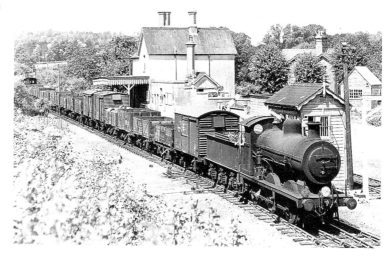

Centre right: By the time this view was taken of Rudgwick Station, on 16 March 1968, all track and signalling facilities had been removed. Today it is still possible to walk along the trackbed at Rudgwick. All the station buildings have disappeared, but the railway cottages on the right of this view remain.
D. A. Idle

Below: An Ivatt Class 2 2-6-2T No 41301 stops at Baynards with the 9.22am Guildford to Horsham train on 13 March 1962. Fortunately the station buildings and platform canopies remain, almost the same in 1996 as when the last train pulled out.
J. Scrace

Above: An Ivatt Class 2 2-6-2T, No 41287, pauses at Cranleigh with the 10.34 Guildford to Horsham train on 1 August 1964. This locomotive was to haul the last train over the line the following year. *J. Scrace*

Below: No 41287 at Guildford station with the 19.34 to Horsham, the last passenger train to use the line, on 12 June 1965. Guildford station has subsequently been extensively rebuilt. *J. Scrace*

Above: No 41325 runs into Southwater station with the 15.21 Horsham to Brighton train on 29 April 1964.
J. C. Haydon

course of the railway has been converted into a road, but the old railway retaining walls and concrete fences remain. Now that the huge cement works at Beeding has closed, the line south of here has also been turned into a footpath, but the sidings at the cement works, which perhaps not unexpectedly were encased in concrete, remain.

A spur at Christ's Hospital, which once allowed a connection to be made between the two lines, was closed in 1867 by the LBSCR, to thwart any ambitions of the LSWR using the two routes to the south coast. Even in later years there were no regular through services from Shoreham-by-Sea to Guildford, connections having to be made at Christ's Hospital or Horsham. Yet today the two routes are connected as never before, as together they provide a railway walk known as the Downs Link, running for many miles from the North Downs near Guildford to the South Downs near Shoreham-by-Sea.

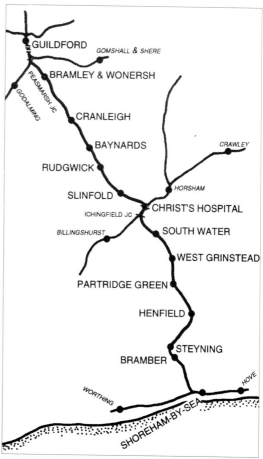

Above: No 41301 pauses at West Grinstead with the 13.30 Brighton to Horsham train on 30 March 1964. *J. Scrace*

Right: Although the station house at Partridge Green was still part occupied when this view was taken on 25 April 1967, a year after closure of the line, the scene is one of abandonment and dereliction. *J. Vaughan*

Below: West Grinstead station, viewed here in April 1995, which now forms part of the Downs Link, a long distance footpath from the North to South Downs. *Author*

12 Memories of Midhurst

Midhurst is located in the wooded Vale of Sussex which provided a natural communications route, and as far back as 1794 the town was served by the Midhurst Canal. Later the London Brighton & South Coast Railway (LBSCR) provided 23 miles of line that followed the canal and east-west course of the River Rother near Pulborough and Petworth, before turning south to connect Midhurst to Chichester. Midhurst was also served by the London & South Western Railway's (LSWR) 9¼-mile route from Petersfield.

The LBSCR line from Hardham Junction at Pulborough to Petworth opened in August 1859. In the opening year an engine ran out of Petworth shed and for over 17 miles towards Horsham, without any crew, before being stopped. The route was extended to Midhurst in October 1866 and a second LBSCR line from Midhurst to Chichester was opened in July 1881. Running south from Midhurst, the line was forced to climb and tunnel through the South Downs. Indeed, near Cocking station one of the highest parts of the South Downs is reached. Of particular interest was the station at Singleton which was heavily engineered into the Downs, with four platforms to serve the nearby Goodwood Racecourse, which itself was laid out on top of the Downs by the Dukes of Richmond. The line then followed the secluded valley of the River Lavant before skirting the western flanks of Chichester.

Both the rival LSWR and the LBSCR had stations

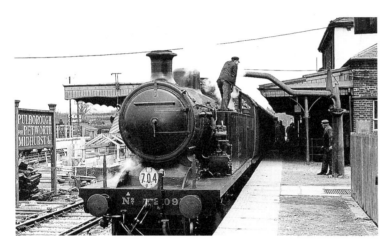

Left: 'Pulborough for Petworth, Midhurst Etc.' the station nameboard asserts as ex-LBSCR Class I3 4-4-2T No 209 takes water on 16 April 1938 in Southern Railway days. The view today, with the exception of the motive power and the rail connections that could once be made here, is surprisingly little changed. *K. O. B. Nichols*

Below: Map of stations at Midhurst in 1938. *Crown Copyright*

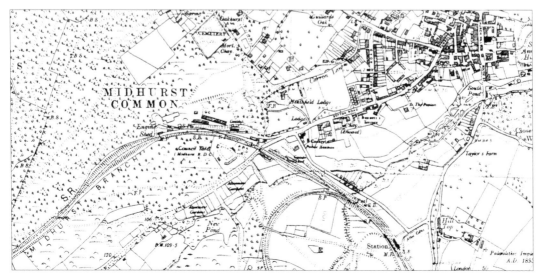

at Midhurst. They were connected in 1866, but there was no through working until the Southern Railway took over. In July 1925 the LSWR former terminal station was closed and all trains diverted to the LBSCR through station. The station was not particu- larly well sited and its inconvenience is said to have helped lead to the early demise of passenger services to the town.

The first line to close to passengers was that from Chichester to Midhurst, as far back as July 1935.

Above: The last train at Petworth. Beside the Class 08 shunter, from left to right, are the station manager from Pulborough; the guard R. Little; the driver H. G. Stokes; and the secondman, R. Holden. The date was 20 May 1966.
J. Vaughan

Left: The station at Fittleworth, viewed from the road approach and in good condition in April 1995.
Author

Left: The last train headed by D3669 prepares to leave Petworth station, bringing to an end 107 years of operating railway history on 20 May 1966. *J. Vaughan*

Below left: Petworth station in use as a private house in April 1995. *Author*

Through freight was truncated by part of the route being washed away in 1951, yet interestingly enough this was the last line to lose all services, as freight remained between Chichester and Lavant until March 1991. The route from Petersfield through Midhurst to Pulborough closed to passengers in February 1955. Freight remained on the Pulborough to Midhurst section until October 1964 and as far as Petworth until May 1966.

The stations on the Pulborough to Midhurst section were of timber construction and their design was not unlike some in Scotland. Both Fittleworth and Petworth remain and are in residential use. Very considerable traces of the route through the Downs from Midhurst to Chichester also remain, the extensive earthworks and steep-sided chalk cuttings being clearly visible. The stations on this line, which were of substantial brick construction and dated 1880, all remain. At Lavant the station has been converted into a housing development, that at Singleton remains and at Cocking the station has been sensitively extended. At Midhurst the station areas have been put to

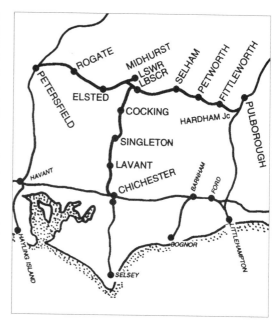

Above: A Class M7 0-4-4T No 30109 on the 12.33pm from Pulborough to Midhurst at Selham station on 15 June 1954.
J. H. Aston

Left: A Class D3 0-6-2T No 2387 with a Midhurst to Horsham train stands at the ex-LBSCR station at Midhurst in April 1947. The typical tile-hung station has since been demolished. Of interest is the platform notice-board that was clearly once used to advertise events at Crystal Palace.
R. Baxter

Below left: An undated, but probably early 1950s, view of Midhurst signalbox. The ex-LBSCR station buildings can just be seen in the background.
Ian Allan Library

Above: An undated view of Cocking station, looking north towards Midhurst, and near the end of its railway use.
Ian Allan Library

Right: A similar view of Cocking station in April 1995. Ornate stonework inscribing the LBSCR initials and 1880 gives a clear indication of the ownership and construction of this station. *Author*

Below right: To the south of Cocking station the line continued its climb before cutting through the South Downs. The north end of this tunnel can be seen here in April 1995. *Author*

various uses including an industrial depot and the LBSCR station buildings have been demolished.

There have been rumours of a possible reopening of the Midhurst to Chichester section. However, the tunnels on the route north from Lavant, because many bricks have become dislodged and gates at one time prevented public entry, now shelter bat colonies which would have to be safely rehoused before any reopening could take place. As it is, the Chichester to Lavant section has already been converted into a footpath with the possibility of this eventually being extended to Midhurst.

13 Secret Hampshire

The county of Hampshire has a considerable military heritage. However, the Woolmer Instructional Railway, to become better known in 1935 as the Longmoor Military Railway, was unique in that it was a series of lines in deepest Hampshire run by the Royal Engineers — to train in the use of running trains! The system dated from 1903 when the British Army established a camp at Longmoor. As it turned out, parts of the area were too wet and the main camp was moved to higher and drier land at Bordon. The camp was soon expanded and the army requested a railway link. The ensuing light railway was opened from Bentley, on the Alton line, to Bordon in December 1905.

By 1908 a military railway linked Longmoor to the Bordon branch. A line also ran south to Liss, although a connection with the main Portsmouth line was not made until 1942. At its peak about 70 miles of track focused on a circular line north of the Longmoor camp. Links from the military-controlled lines to Liss in the south and, by crossing under the A325 at Whitehill, to Bordon to the north were retained for flexibility. Some lines were for freight, others were for training purposes only, and signalling and other equipment was provided to give a full range of instruction for specialist officers in the Royal Engineers in railway operation.

The system was very heavily used in both World Wars and became the main railway training centre for the British Army. Yet it became increasingly recognised that in strategic warfare, whilst railways could speed troops and equipment close to the battle zone, movement from thereon by rail could be difficult. Consequently the development of all-purpose road army vehicles and the reduced size of the army after World War 2 meant that the training requirement for the military railway was reduced.

Passenger services on the Bordon branch ended in September 1957 and the military connection, together with the Bordon branch, closed completely in April 1966. Diesels replaced steam and the British Army's last steam locomotive to operate on the network was named *Errol Lonsdale* in January 1968. Before closure of the remainder of the railway, which had already been reduced from its peak mileage, the system became home for preserved locomotives and there were open days for enthusiasts which were very popular. The line was also used for filming purposes and in 1966 The Great St Trinians Train Robbery involved sequences that may not have been tolerated

Below: The 13.17 service to Liss awaits at Longmoor Downs station on an open day on 3 June 1967, with an 'Austerity' 0-6-0ST No 196, later named *Errol Lonsdale*, at the head of two ex-SECR 'birdcage' carriages. *J. H. Bird*

by BR. The remaining passenger services and connection to Liss closed in October 1969, although total closure to freight was not until 1971.

The diary records an open day on the LMR:

28 September 1968: At Godalming the bridge was washed away and a bus service connected with the stations each side. The Longmoor Military Railway was packed with enthusiasts. It felt strange running into War Department property, but the ride was very interesting; there were lots of different steam engines to see. I was so carried away photographing the engines on the LMR that I suddenly saw my return train to London pull into the BR station at Liss. I scrambled over the hedge and just caught it in time.

Fortunately once the system closed the steam locomotives and some of the rolling stock associated with the line went into preservation. Today an extensive display of items relating to the history of the

Above: WD 2-10-0 No 600 *Gordon*, built in 1943, eases the first train of the Longmoor Military Railway's open day of 28 September 1968, the 10.15 Longmoor Downs to Liss, over the LMR yard bridge.
J. H. Bird

Left: Abandoned railway facilities near Longmoor Downs, once the main station on the network, in April 1995.
Author's collection

Above: The disused trackbed curving towards the site of the Longmoor Military Railway yard bridge in April 1995. *Author's collection*

Below: A Longmoor Military Railway open day on 5 July 1969. The single line token is exchanged at Liss Forest Road. On closure of the LMR the locomotive *Gordon* passed into preservation. *M. Mullins*

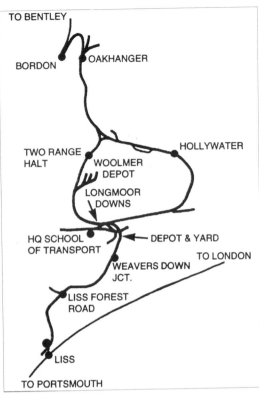

Longmoor Military Railway is to be found at the Museum of Army Transport at Beverley in Yorkshire. Longmoor Camp remains in army use, but there are no tracks or trains. Improvements to the A3 have made use of part of the old line, but many traces still remain. The old control room can still be seen beside the road at Longmoor, together with other buildings once associated with the railway. The route of the line leading to Bordon remains clearly visible, although the station at Bordon is now an industrial estate. At Liss part of the track near the main line station has been turned into a footpath, but the original LMR platform and waiting shelter remain.

Above left: The overgrown Longmoor Military Railway station platform at Liss in April 1995. The LMR station was located adjacent to that on the main London to Portsmouth line.
Author

Above right: The Longmoor Military Railway, after closure, awaits the demolition contractor at Oakhanger station on 4 July 1971.
A. Jackson

Right: The very substantial end of the line buffer block at Liss, still *in situ* in April 1995.
Author

14 A ghost on the way to Gosport

The line from Alton that ran south to Fareham was known as the Meon Valley line. The 22¼-mile route ran from Butts Junction, south of Alton, through attractive and remote Hampshire countryside following the River Meon for much of its route to Knowle Junction north of Fareham. The line opened in June 1903 and was one of the last substantial railway routes built in this country. At Fareham it was possible to continue 4¼ miles to Gosport on an earlier line first opened in 1841. The Tuscan colonnaded station at Gosport was designed by Sir William Tite and is particularly attractive. For a time Queen Victoria used this station on her trips to the Isle of Wight.

Stations on the Meon Valley line were built to a sizeable scale with extensive platforms in the expectation that they would be served by main line trains to Gosport and Stokes Bay. As it turned out, traffic never developed as anticipated. With electrification ending at Alton in 1937, through running was limited, whilst Gosport was conveniently served from Portsmouth Harbour.

The link to Gosport closed to passengers in June 1953 and the Meon Valley line closed to passenger traffic in February 1955. Freight continued from Fareham to Droxford until 1962 and on a northern section from Alton to Farringdon until 1968. Experiments with a railcar on a part of the Meon Valley route were short-lived, but freight to Fort Brockhurst on the Gosport section lasted until 1995.

Below: The Southern Railway acquired 14 American-built 0-6-0T locomotives which passed into BR stock and spent most of their time at the docks in Southampton. Here 'USA' 0-6-0T No 30064 is in steam at Droxford which was for a time the terminus of the line from Fareham in the Meon Valley. This view was taken on 17 November 1968 on a 'hush-hush' trip on the line. No 30064 is now preserved on the Bluebell Railway. *J. H. Bird*

Top right: Sadler's rail coach, the light railcar which was on trials on a privately owned part of the Meon Valley branch after it closed. It was hoped such a service would be used between Smallbrook Junction and Cowes on the Isle of Wight, but unfortunately it was not to be. *AEC*

Right: The approach to the forbidding and derelict station at Privett on 11 February 1962. *L. Sandler*

Below: The northern entrance of Meon Tunnel, securely safeguarded against intruders on a cold day on 18 February 1985. *Author*

Left: The unique metal construction of West Meon Viaduct in the course of dismantling for scrap in March 1957.
Hugh Davies

Centre left: Class 33 No D6515 arrives at Gosport on 9 September 1968 with the daily branch freight from Fareham.
J. H. Bird

Below: Gosport station in the morning sunlight on 31 October 1968. Considerable parcels traffic (84,000 parcels in 1966) used the station up to its closure in 1969.
A. McIntyre

Top right: The same wall of Gosport station remaining in September 1995, long after fire, disuse and demolition had turned the building into a ruin.
Author

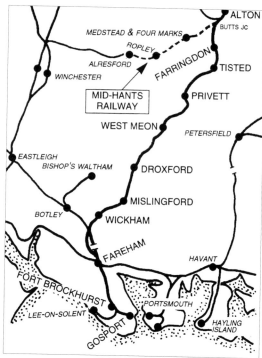

Gosport — following the reopening of the line to Mansfield — is arguably one of Britain's largest towns not served directly by a railway.

Yet it was in the Meon Valley where a fascinating incident is set, at the remote and isolated 1,058yd tunnel at Privett. I am not convinced that there are ghosts, but I will leave the reader to weigh the evidence in this case. The diary clearly records:

18 February 1985: A cold and snowy day, but until I reached the tunnel at Privett all had gone well. I had photographed Meon Tunnel and left the car with the intention of photographing Privett Tunnel's northern portal. However, try as I would, I could not get down to the old trackbed. In the end with snow flurries adding to my discomfort, I felt particularly cold and took what photographs I could and abandoned my quest.

When the photographs were subsequently developed those of Privett Tunnel had all manner of odd shapes and colours on them, but fortunately they were not destroyed. A few years later I stumbled upon a book of ghost stories; it told the tale that at the time the tunnel was constructed someone had been killed and it was claimed that the tunnel was haunted. I sought out the photographs and there it was, the ghost of Privett Tunnel.

Left: The imposing frontage of Gosport station, for a time used by Queen Victoria on her trips to the Isle of Wight. The station was designed by Sir William Tite and built in 1841. It lost its roof by fire in World War 2, but it is a listed building and the attractive Tuscan colonnade and stylish iron railings remain and are particularly fine. This view was taken in September 1995. *Author*

15 The last train over Langstone Bridge

The 4½-mile line from Havant, on the main London to Portsmouth line, to Hayling Island opened as far as Langston (for many years the spelling excluded the final 'e') for freight in January 1865, but not throughout until July 1867. Originally it was planned that the line should run on an embankment built across the shallow waters of Langston Harbour to save buying land on the island. However, the causeway across the sea was soon damaged by storms. Consequently a bridge to the mainland, with the line running along the flat western coast of the island, was decided upon for the final route.

Part of the original plan was to run services from Langston Harbour to the well-protected Bembridge Harbour on the eastern coast of the Isle of Wight, but this service operated only for a short time between 1882 and 1888 and the line was in financial trouble for many years. Hayling Island was a popular destination during the peak summer season, and in its heyday crowds of trippers made their way to the coast. At one time, in the summer peak, a 15min interval service was provided. It was also one of the quieter south coast resorts, particularly in winter, when trains of one coach were often sufficient.

The Langston Railway Bridge was constructed mainly in timber with the lower parts encased in concrete, although a metal opening section was provided over the deepest water for boats using Langston Harbour. As with the original road bridge, where tolls were once paid to the railway and buses were forced to limit the number of their passengers, a weight restriction on the rail bridge also meant that few classes of locomotive could be used on the branch. For many years the famous ex-LBSCR 'Terrier' class of locomotive, which were based at the nearby Fratton shed, but which still weighed 28 tons, were almost exclusively used on the route. At one period they were fitted with spark arresters, from former use in Newhaven Docks, but which also helped to avert incinerating the mainly wooden Langston Bridge.

The line was an attractive backwater, remaining independent until Southern Railway days. It was never electrified, retaining steam traction to the end. Unfortunately it had limited numbers of winter passengers and it therefore perhaps came as no great surprise when it closed in November 1963. It was a much-loved branch line and attempts were made at preservation. Regretfully they were not successful, but today, although much of the line was relatively lightly constructed, many traces of the route and the footings of Langston Bridge can still be seen. Indeed, part of the line south of Langston Bridge recalls memories of the railway and its engines by being called the Hayling Billy cycle route.

Below: An LBSCR 'Terrier' No 635 with a passenger train crossing the opening section of Langston Bridge, clearly early in the line's operation. *M. E. Ware*

Right: 'Terrier' No 32650 crosses Langston Bridge with the 12.55pm Hayling Island to Havant train on the last day of service, 2 November 1963.
Brian Stephenson

Below: 'Terrier' No 32650 comes off Langston Bridge with the 1.35pm Havant to Hayling Island train, on the last day of service 2 November 1963.
Brian Stephenson

Above: 'Terrier' No 32650 leaves Langston with the 2.20pm from Havant to Hayling Island, again on the last day of service 2 November 1963.
P. Paye

Left: The remains of the former halt at Langston, the target of vandals, in August 1969. The track used to continue across the road in the background by means of a level crossing, long since removed.
J. H. Bird

Below: 1 March 1967 and the Hayling Island branch was being lifted. Here a truck is loaded with sleepers at the branch's bay platform at Havant.
J. Vaughan

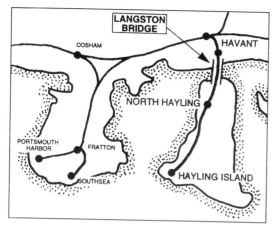

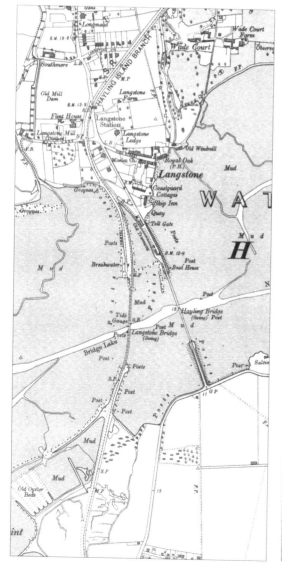

Above: The gaunt signal post remaining at the south end of Langston Bridge was clearly used as a vantage point to photograph trains coming off the bridge.

Photographed here on 25 June 1985, the signal post still remained *in situ* 10 years later. *Author*

Left: Map of Langston Bridge 1942. *Crown Copyright*

Below: Just the concrete bases of Langston Bridge and the substantial metal swing mechanism support remained in August 1995. *Author*

16 Links to the lost liners

The Pilgrim Fathers set sail in 1620 for Plymouth and America from the port of Southampton in the 180-ton Mayflower. Little were they to realise that in future years Southampton was to become the main transatlantic sea route to America. Indeed the 46,329-ton luxury ocean liner *Titanic* sailed on its doomed maiden voyage in 1912 from this port. The location is unique in that Southampton's position on the Solent provides for double high tides with little change in the intervening 2hr of high water. This was to prove beneficial as the size of ships increased, and Southampton was to rival and later eclipse Liverpool as a port.

The London & Southampton Railway built a particularly elegant terminus in Southampton following the opening of the line throughout from London in June 1839. Designed by Sir William Tite it was in a stuccoed Italianate classical style with a stone arcade at its

Left: The original Southampton Terminus station in November 1985, almost 20 years after passenger closure, with restoration just about to commence. It was perhaps fitting that the building was turned into a casino as the directors of the original London & Southampton Railway also gambled that their venture would be a success. The Italianate design has some affinity with nearby Regency housing. The extension to the former South Western Hotel is the building towering in the background. *Author*

Above: Class D1 4-4-0 No 31735 at Southampton Terminus with the 10.57am Salisbury to Portsmouth and Southsea parcels train on 4 February 1961.
J. C. Haydon

Left centre: In later years the main entrance to the South Western Hotel was from the Terminus station. Apart from the Doric style columns, the stonework incorporated locomotive wheels from the Southern Railway arms. The building remains in office use, as this view taken in May 1995 shows.
Author

Far left: The rear and side of the Terminus station, in May 1995, still retains part of the overall roof which was extended in the 1920s when the original station was amalgamated with extensions to the adjacent hotel.
Author

Left: The imposing façade of the former South Western Hotel at Southampton in May 1995. The station was located to the rear of the hotel building. *Author*

front. From that time onwards Southampton and its docks were to experience a period of continuous expansion.

After obtaining powers to build a line to Portsmouth, the London & Southampton railway changed its title to become the well-known London and South Western Railway. This company purchased the docks in 1892 and they were developed and improved. The LSWR also completed the substantial South Western hotel close to their original terminus. Designed by John Norton in a French Renaissance style it was fully operational by 1872 and provided accommodation for liner passengers. High on the Canute Road elevation is a relief of Queen Victoria, with boats and trains. In all respects it contrasted with the design and scale of the original terminus. An extension to the hotel in the 1920s was of equally contrasting design.

The Southern Railway, as later owners of Southampton Docks, planned for a completely modern Ocean Terminal built beside the deep water area at the confluence of the Rivers Test and Itchen. With spacious waiting and refreshment facilities, two tracks led into the 'station' building which was

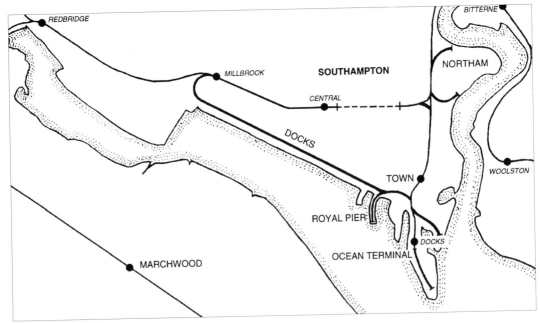

FIRST SAILING of R.M.S. "QUEEN MARY"
from SOUTHAMPTON
WEDNESDAY, 27th. MAY

COMBINED RAIL & SEAT TICKETS — Including Rail from WATERLOO at 1.18 p.m. and reserved seat at SOUTHAMPTON DOCKS **10/6** (Children 5/3)

COMBINED RAIL & STEAMER TICKETS — Including Rail from VICTORIA at 10.45 am EAST CROYDON 11.1 am to NEWHAVEN and CRUISE down the Channel to SOUTHAMPTON WATER **25/-** (Children 12/6)

BOOKINGS ALSO FROM CERTAIN SUBURBAN STATIONS.

TICKETS STRICTLY LIMITED.
BOOK IN ADVANCE AT STATIONS.

Ask for handbill giving full details
at S.R. Stations.

SOUTHERN RAILWAY'S SOUTHAMPTON DOCKS

Left: A Southern Railway poster announcing the maiden voyage of the *Queen Mary.* Cunard's brand-new ship sailed for New York for the first time in May 1936. *Courtesy NRM*

Centre: The Ocean Liner Terminal was opened by Clement Attlee in 1950. A rather plain exterior belied its magnificent and spacious 'Odeon'-style interior, as this view of the first class reception hall shows. It was nevertheless demolished in 1983. *British Transport Commission*

Bottom: The *Queen Mary* photographed at Southampton Docks on 26 April 1967. After 1,001 crossings of the Atlantic and 31 years' service the *Queen Mary* left Southampton for the last time in October that year. *Author*

designed, yet again, in a contrasting modern style. The plain exterior belied the interior which was particularly opulent, designed to rival any airport departure lounge. However, World War 2 intervened and the terminal did not open until July 1950. Consequently it had only a very short heyday before the airlines really stole the transatlantic passenger traffic.

Although the docks continue to expand, there have been changes. The South Western Hotel closed in 1940, yet it was nonetheless restored and reopened as offices after World War 2. The terminus station closed in September 1966, but much of the original station building has been restored. The Ocean Liner Terminal was demolished in 1983. Its loss has been in common with many of the great ocean liners and the 'Ocean Liner Express' trains that ran to the dockside. Yet fortunately it is still possible to travel directly by rail from London to the Eastern Docks at Southampton, including on special trips provided by the 'Orient Express' restored Pullman coaches such as *Ibis, Ione* and *Zena,* that in a previous life were in fact all used on the 'Ocean Liner Expresses'.

Furthermore, it is still possible to catch an ocean liner to America where the *Queen Mary*, that most elegant of ocean liners, is preserved and where incidentally America's own Southern Railway ran under that name until 1990.

The end of an era

The comparatively mild climate, scenic attractions, sandy beaches and relatively easy access did much to establish the Isle of Wight as a holiday destination. Cowes, once the main gateway to the island, remains world famous for yachting; Newport, Ryde, Shanklin and Ventnor all expanded in Victorian times from villages to fashionable towns and resorts. In fact the present development pattern of the Isle of Wight has been influenced by the railways. At one time a 2½-mile railway tunnel was proposed under the Solent to the Freshwater line which, if built, may have changed the emphasis of development on the island.

Queen Victoria loved the island and purchased the Osborne estate in 1845 as a holiday retreat. Many years later, in January 1901, she died here and there is something very 'final' about Osborne. It marked the end of an era, the British Empire had reached its greatest extent and in some respects also the railways; no further lines were built on the island after Victoria's death.

The development on the island of a network of about 50 miles of mainly single-line railways was surprisingly complicated. Five independent and often rival railway companies were involved. The first line to be opened, in June 1862, ran from Cowes to Newport. This was followed by a line from St John's Road at Ryde to Shanklin in August 1864, which was extended to Ventnor two years later. A line from Sandown to the outskirts of Newport opened in October 1875, together with a second link from Smallbrook Junction to Newport later in that year. A new line from Ryde St John's Road to Ryde Pier was opened in July 1880. The convenience provided by this link was to make Ryde the main gateway to the Island. The Bembridge branch opened in May 1882 and passenger traffic began on the Newport to Freshwater route by July 1889. The last line to be built was the alternative route to Ventnor Town, later more realistically called Ventnor West, which opened from Merstone as far as St Lawrence in July 1897. The extension to the outskirts of Ventnor in June 1900 completed the island's network.

Although built to standard gauge, the island's railways were always distinctive. The physical separation from the mainland and the constricted loading gauge meant that much of the mainland stock was not suitable for use on the island. Thus it was that in 1923 the Southern Railway took over a rather run-down network. Improvements were made, a resident manager installed and holiday traffic was encouraged by the Southern, even though it was interrupted by World

War 2. After the war little general freight was carried, but the substantial peak holiday traffic continued, particularly on summer Saturdays.

Left: An Isle of Wight poster showing the co-operation between the IW Railway and the IW Central Railway in promoting the island. The landscapes of the 'Garden Isle' shown on the poster, unlike the railways, have undergone little significant change. *Courtesy NRM*

Below left: Class 02 0-4-4T No 18 *Ningwood* crosses the River Medina as it storms out of Newport with the 14.24 Cowes to Ryde train on 17 June 1965.
M. Dunnett

Above: A railway ticket to Ryde inevitably still leads to a trip on the pier. Here Class 02 0-4-4T No 16 *Ventnor* is seen running light along the listed Ryde Pier on 19 June 1965. *M. Dunnett*

Below: In its Southern livery, this view of an 0-6-0T 'Terrier' on the Isle of Wight, No 8 *Freshwater*, leaving Merstone on a sunny day in June 1945 for Ventnor West, in many ways typifies the heyday of the island's railways. *Real Photos*

The winds of change

Yet the summer peak was offset by months of meagre winter traffic and nationalisation saw cutbacks. There had already been closure of the Ventnor West, Freshwater and Bembridge lines by the early 1950s when the first demands came in the for closure of the entire network. By the 1960s the remaining lines had become neglected and the Beeching Report again proposed total closure. In 1964 closure proposals for the remainder of the system were published.

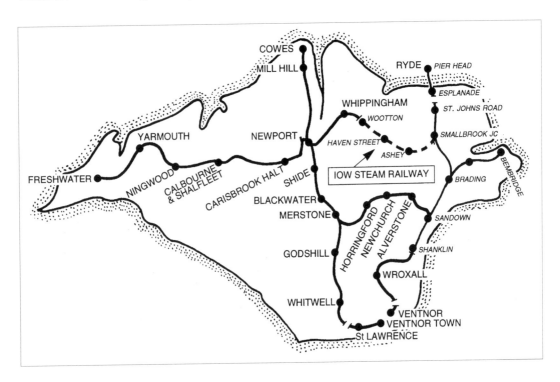

Left: Suddenly most of the island's railways were gone! The preserved Class 02 0-4-4T No 24 *Calbourne* shunts in the overgrown and disused yard at Newport. Once called the Clapham Junction of the island, this was hardly the case on 24 November 1970. *J. Goss*

Right: The train headed by No 24 *Calbourne* on 24 January 1971 is cautiously eased through a cutting near Wootton station where the shifting clay had pushed the track out of alignment and reduced clearances to an absolute minimum. *Dr J. Mackett*

Below: The island's railways have very many friends. Huge crowds watch No 24 *Calbourne* set out from Newport station with preserved stock for Havenstreet. This was the first train for over four years to run, on 24 January 1971, and sadly the last for many years between Wootton and Newport as the track was torn up a few days after the special had passed. *Dr J. Mackett*

A fierce battle was fought by a devoted following and the problems of dispersing thousands of peak summer tourists along the almost ½-mile long Ryde Pier, with ferries arriving at 15min intervals, led to a reprieve. Nevertheless all remaining services were closed by April 1966 with the exception of the Ryde to Shanklin line. This last 8½-mile section was electrified and reopened with second-hand London tube stock which was used to overcome the loading gauge restrictions.

Although some of the earlier closures may have been justified — for example Ventnor perhaps could not really justify two independent stations — yet the remaining Ventnor station generated a vast amount of traffic for the wider network. It is consequently sometimes alleged that its closure and the retention of the Ryde to Shanklin section was a cynical ploy, in that the remaining line, without the advantage of Ventnor, would not be commercially viable and could soon also be closed.

Fortunately a transformation in opinion continues to develop. Not only would the closure of the Ryde to Shanklin route now be unthinkable, there is ever growing pressure to reinstate the southern section to Ventnor. In addition, in January 1971 locomotive No 24 *Calbourne* and some rolling stock, that had been saved from being scrapped, were moved from a dilapidated Newport station to Havenstreet. Today the section from Smallbrook Junction to Wootton has been reopened as the Isle of Wight Steam Railway (the route was sensibly identified in the island's structure plan). There are plans to return once again to Newport, where in the future connection may even possibly be made with a narrow gauge railway to Cowes in the north. Consequently in the longer term the bulk of the island's key settlements may once again be served by rail. Finally, of course, it is still possible to buy a railway ticket to Ryde!

Above: The signalbox and station nameplate still remained, damaged but largely intact at Cowes station on 6 August 1971. The footbridge was later salvaged for use on the Mid-Hants Railway. *G. Merrin*

Below: Ventnor Town station 1909. *Crown Copyright*

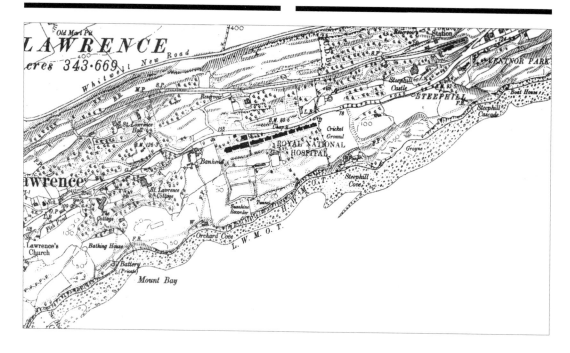

Above: At Newport the trackbed from Cowes passed a fallen 10¼ milepost and an old signal post before suddenly becoming part of a road, as this view taken on 6 August 1971 shows. *G. Merrin*

Left: The southern portal of the tunnel from Wroxall at Ventnor, viewed here in August 1986. All is currently quiet, but in the 1950s up to 5,000 passengers could alight at the station in a single day. The tunnel is 1,312yd long and falls at 1 in 173 towards Ventnor station to arrive at this southern portal some 276ft above sea level. *Author*

Above right: The tunnel on the alternative line to Ventnor, via St Lawrence, has been turned into a mushroom farm as this view of the northern portal, taken in August 1986, shows. The tunnel is 619yd long, falling at a grade of 1 in 55. *Author*

Centre right: A short tunnel led to a quarry at Ashey Down; the northern portal was still visible, amidst the rubbish, when this view was taken in August 1986. *Author*

Bottom right: The railways live on in the Isle of Wight! Not only the remaining line from Shanklin to Ryde, but also the preserved line currently running from Smallbrook Junction to Wootton. Here Class O2 0-4-4T *Calbourne*, which was built in 1891, awaits departure from Havenstreet; the scene could well be from many years past, but it was in fact taken on Whit Monday 1971.
J. H. Bird

18 All change for the coast

The London & South Western Railway's main line from London to Exeter provided many connections for nearby towns. West of Chard Junction, a number of junctions once provided access to the sea. The first of these was at Axminster where the 6¾-mile Axminster & Lyme Regis Light Railway was worked by the LSWR from its opening in August 1903. The topography of these parts is particularly precipitous and the railway was forced to twist and turn with considerable gradients and earthworks in order to link the main line to the coast. For many years, including BR days right up until 1961, the line was operated by attractive LSWR Adams-designed Radial tank engines. These were able to cope with the heavy grades and sharp curvature, although three coaches required double-heading.

Lyme Regis is now primarily a holiday resort, embracing the 600ft Cobb, which has become famous for its literary and film settings. Yet the Cobb's original purpose was to aid the development of Lyme Regis as a fishing port. As a port, the Cobb was used to import cement to build the massive Cannington Viaduct on the outskirts of Lyme Regis.

The line had only one intermediate station at Combpyne. This had some tourist traffic to the nearby countryside and coastal landslip, but was located in a remote area some considerable distance from the settlement of Combpyne and traffic was not heavy. The line was single throughout and the only crossing loop, at Combpyne, was taken out in 1930.

Although there was peak summer traffic, Lyme Regis has remained a small and relatively remote coastal town. Through coaches were provided from Waterloo, but travel to the town mostly involved a change of trains at Axminster. The station at Lyme Regis was situated high above the settlement and some distance from the sea, where the beach is partly shingle. Consequently, and many would say fortunately, holiday traffic and the town itself never grew to the extent of some south coast resorts.

Diesel trains were introduced in the early 1960s, but in winter traffic could be sparse and the route was not unexpectedly identified for withdrawal of passenger services in the Beeching Report. It closed in November 1965, freight having ended the previous year. Although the line itself has by now long since closed, much remains. One of the attractive LSWR Adams-designed Radial tanks that were such a feature of the route for so many years, has been preserved on the Bluebell Railway. After closure, the largely wooden station buildings at Combpyne were transferred for use on the Mid-Hants line, although the station house remains. Many earthworks associated with the old line are also still clearly visible in the landscape, including the vast Cannington Viaduct. Lyme Regis station is currently used as an industrial area.

Below: Axminster station in Southern Railway days on 25 May 1935. Awaiting with the branch train is an ex-LSWR Radial tank 4-4-2T No 3126, whilst Nos 3520 and 455 are seen in the main platforms.
H. C. Casserley

An extract from the diary states:

11 August 1966: There were quite a few passengers at Sidmouth Junction where I caught the train for Yeovil Junction. At Axminster the rusting line to Lyme Regis could still be seen curving round and over the main line. Changing from Yeovil Junction to Yeovil Town was interesting because the Town station was huge, but only used by a single-coach train. However, the service was quite full.

Axminster station and its attractive main stone building remains open. Sidmouth Junction, after closure in March 1967, reopened as Feniton. A three-mile section of the Seaton line is used by electric trams and there are persistent murmurings of an eventual reopening of the Lyme Regis line.

Above: An ex-LSWR Radial tank No 30582 heads a single coach of happy holidaymakers on the switchback and steeply-graded Lyme Regis branch in 1961. *Ian Allan Library*

Left: The derelict Lyme Regis platform at Axminster station in September 1995. The attractive main buildings dating from 1859 remain, but the footbridge and signalbox have long since gone. *Author*

Above: The 11.34am from Lyme Regis in the deep cutting approaching Combpyne hauled by Radial tank No 30582. *S. C. Nash*

Left: Ex-LSWR Radial tank No 30583 crosses Cannington Viaduct with the 11.37am Lyme Regis to Axminster train on 3 June 1959. Note the jack arch inserted as a result of subsidence to part of the concrete structure. *J. H. Aston*

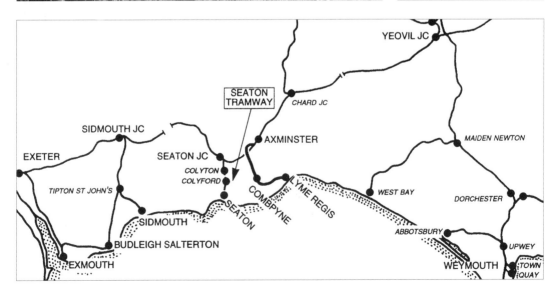

Above: Ex-LMS Ivatt Class 2 2-6-2T No 41291 crossing Cannington Viaduct with the 11.42am Lyme Regis to Axminster train on 6 March 1965. The subsidence problems with the viaduct can clearly be seen in this view. *G. Robinson*

Right: Detail of the brick-built jack arch, inserted within the third concrete span to prevent further subsidence of Cannington Viaduct. The solution seems to have arrested any further subsidence, but the absence of trains over the viaduct may also have helped! *Author*

Below: Cannington Viaduct remains an impressive feature in the landscape, as this view taken in September 1995 shows. *Author*

Table 36 YEOVIL JUNCTION and YEOVIL TOWN

Miles	Down	MX	A	am	am	am	P	SX	SO	SX	SO	SX	SO	J	SO	J	SX	SO	H	SO	pm	SO	J	pm	D
	Week Days																								
	Yeovil Junction . dep	4J35	5 8	7 36	8 7	8 35	9 12	9 45	1020	1035	11 3	1115	1142	12 2	1230	1235	1255	1 15	2 9	2 46	3 10	3 35	3 53	4 33	5 17
1¾	Yeovil Town .. arr	4J40	5 13	7 40	8 11	8 39	9 16	9 49	1024	1039	11 7	1119	1146	12 6	1234	1240	1259	1 19	2 13	2 50	3 14	3 40	3 57	4 37	5 21

Down	pm	pm	pm	pm	pm	pm	FO	pm	pm	pm		am	am	am	pm	pm	pm	pm	pm	pm	pm	pm	pm	pm	pm
	Week Days—continued											**Sundays**													
Yeovil Junction. dep	5 35	6 5	6 33	7 14	7 55	8 25	8 42	8 56	9 40	1121	..	4 24	5 33	1120	1243	1 10	2 22	3 5	5 21	6 16	6 48	8 56	9 10	11 2	1130
Yeovil Town .. arr	5 39	6 9	6 37	7 18	7 59	8 29	8 47	9 0	9 44	1126	....	4 29	5 38	1124	1247	1 14	2 26	3 9	5 25	6 20	6 52	9 0	9 15	11 6	1135

Miles	Up	am	am	am	D	am	R	am	SX	SO	SX	SO	SX	SO	SX	SO	J	SO	SX	SO	SO	H	SO	T	pm	pm
	Week Days																									
	Yeovil Town .. dep	6 25	6 31	6 55	7 50	7 56	8 8	8 20	8 55	9 8	9 28	1010	1025	1050	11 5	1120	1145	1219	1238	1 5	1 40	1 50	2 30	2 45	3 30	4 6
1¾	Yeovil Junction. arr	6 30	6 35	7 0	7 55	8 0	8 13	8 24	8 59	9 12	9 32	1014	1029	1054	11 9	1124	1149	1223	1242	1 9	1 45	1 54	2 34	2 49	3 34	4 11

Up	pm	D	pm	pm	pm	pm	pm	pm	pm	pm		am	am	am	am	pm	pm	pm	pm	pm	pm	pm	pm	pm	pm	pm
	Week Days—continued											**Sundays**														
Yeovil Town .. dep	4 19	5 5	5 26	5 53	6 20	7 1	7 40	8 10	8 40	9 22	..	7 10	1010	11 5	1148	1235	1 0	2 6	2 45	3 45	5 10	5 48	6 33	7 0	8 40	1050
Yeovil Junction. arr	4 23	5 9	5 30	5 57	6 24	7 5	7 44	8 15	8 44	9 26	....	7 15	1015	11 9	1153	1239	1 4	2 10	2 49	3 50	5 14	5 52	6 37	7 5	8 44	1054

A 4 minutes later on Saturdays **D** 5 minutes *earlier* on Saturdays **FO** Fridays only **H** 6 minutes later on Saturdays
J 7 minutes later on Saturdays **MX** Tuesdays to Fridays **P** 9 minutes later on Saturdays **R** Saturdays only
2nd July to 27th August **SO** Saturdays only **SX** Mondays to Fridays **T** 11 minutes later on Saturdays

Table 37 CHARD JUNCTION and CHARD CENTRAL

Miles	Down	am	am	am	pm	SO	pm	pm	pm	pm
	Week Days only									
	Chard Junction. dep	7 40	8 28	1056	1 0	3 20	5 4	5 50	7 7	9 30
3¼	Chard Central . arr	7 49	8 37	11 6	1 10	3 29	5 13	5 59	7 16	9 39

Miles	Up	am	am	am	pm	SO	pm	pm	pm	pm
	Week Days only									
	Chard Central . dep	7 15	8 10	9 34	12 5	1 52	4 10	5 36	6 9	8 43
3¼	Chard Junction. arr	7 23	8 18	9 42	1213	2 0	4 18	5 44	6 17	8 51

SO Saturdays only

Table 38 AXMINSTER and LYME REGIS

Miles	Down	SO	SX	SO	SO	SX	SO		SX	SO	SX	SO		SX	SO	SX		SO	pm		SO	pm	pm
	Week Days																						
	Axminster . .. dep	8 32	8 40	9 35	1035	1040	11A35	..	1233	1245	1 38	1T50	..	2 48	3 40	4T43	..	4 43	5 40	..	6 47	8 55	9Y45
4½	Combpyne	8 45	8 53	9 48	1048	1053	11A48	....	1246	1258	1 51	2T 3	....	3 1	3 53	4T56	....	4 56	5 53	....	7 0	9 8	....
6¾	Lyme Regis .. arr	8 53	9 1	9 56	1056	11 1	11A56	..	1254	1 6	1 59	2T11	..	3 9	4 1	5T 4	..	5 4	6 1	..	7 8	9 16	10Y 8

Miles	Up	am	SO	SX		SO	SX	SO		SO	SX	SO		SX	SO		SX	SO	SX	SO	pm		pm	pm
	Week Days																							
	Lyme Regis .. dep	7Y18	8 0	8 9	..	9B 0	10 0	10 5	..	11 5	11T37	1210	..	1 10	1 12	..	2 16	3T 5	3 55	4 10	5 10	.	6 7	8 22
2¼	Combpyne	....	8 8	8 17	....	9B 8	10 8	1013	....	1113	11T45	1218	....	1 18	1 20	....	2 24	3T13	4 3	4 18	5 18	...	6 15	8 30
6¾	Axminster . .. arr	7Y40	8 21	8 30	..	9B21	1021	1026	..	1126	11T58	1231	..	1 31	1 33	..	2 37	3T26	4 16	4 31	5 31	.	6 28	8 43

Down	am	pm	pm	pm	pm	pm	pm	pm	pm	pm	pm
Sundays											
Axminster . .. dep	1111	12 6	1 0	2 23	3 20	4 25	5 50	7 18	8 22	9 25	1025
Combpyne	1124	1219	1 13	2 36	3 33	4 38	6 3	7 31	8 35	9 38	1038
Lyme Regis .. arr	1132	1227	1 21	2 44	3 41	4 46	6 11	7 39	8 43	9 46	1046

Up	am	am	pm	pm	pm	pm	pm	pm	pm	pm	pm
Sundays											
Lyme Regis .. dep	1040	1137	1233	1 50	2 50	3 55	4 56	6 45	7 50	8 50	9 50
Combpyne	1048	1145	1241	1 58	2 58	4 3	5 4	6 53	7 58	8 58	9 58
Axminster ... arr	11 1	1158	1254	2 11	3 11	4 16	5 17	7 6	8 11	9 11	1011

A Through Carriages from Waterloo until 27th August **B** Through Carriages to Waterloo 2nd July to 27th August
FO Fridays only **SO** Saturdays only **SX** Mondays to Fridays **T** Through Carriages to or from Waterloo
Y By Southern National Omnibus between Axminster Station and Lyme Regis (Langfords Shop) Times subject to alteration

Table 39 SEATON JUNCTION and SEATON

Miles	Down	am	SO	SX	SO	SX	SO	SX	SO	K	SX	SX	SO	SO	SX	SO	T	SO	SX	SO	pm	pm	pm	pm	pm	F
	Week Days																									
	Seaton Jn... dep	8 5	8 40	8 45	9 42	9 46	1035	1045	11A25	11T40	12 3	1236	1258	1T53	2 5	2 6	2 55	3 20	3 25	4 0	4 48	5 36	6 51	7 55	8 44	9 42
1¼	Colyton	8 9	8 44	8 49	9 46	9 50	1039	1049	11A29	....	12 7	1240	1 2	....	2 9	2 10	2 59	3 24	3 29	4 4	4 52	5 40	6 55	7 59	8 48	9 46
2½	Colyford	8 12	8 47	8 52	9 49	9 53	1042	1052	11A32	—	1210	1243	1 5	..	2 12	2 13	3 2	3 27	3 32	4 7	4 57	5 45	7 0	8 4	8 53	9 51
4¼	Seaton .. .. arr	8 15	8 50	8 55	9 52	9 56	1045	1055	11A37	11T50	1213	1246	1 8	2T 5	2 15	2 16	3 5	3 30	3 35	4 10	5 1	5 49	7 4	8 8	8 57	9 55

Miles	Up	am	am	SO	SX	SO	SX	SO	SO	SX	SO	SX	SO	SX	SX	SO	SO	SO	SX	SO	pm	pm	pm	pm	F
	Week Days																								
	Seaton . .. dep	7 46	8X28	9§ 0	9 18	9 55	10T 5	10T20	1058	1143	12 5	1216	1 26	1 35	2 30	2T35	2 48	3 40	3 48	4 20	5 8	6 10	7 35	8 15	9 23
1¾	Colyford	7 51	8X33	....	9 23	10 0	10T10	....	11 3	1148	1210	1221	1 31	1 42	2 35	....	2 53	3 45	3 53	4 25	5 15	6 17	7 42	8 22	9 30
2¾	Colyton	7 55	8X37	9§ 7	9 27	10 4	10T14	..	11 7	1152	1214	1225	1 35	1 46	2 39	..	2 57	3 49	4 0	4 31	5 20	6 22	7 47	8 27	9 35
4¼	Seaton Jn... arr	7 59	8X41	9§11	9 31	10 8	10T18	10T31	1111	1156	1218	1229	1 39	1 50	2 43	2T46	3 1	3 53	4 6	4 36	5 24	6 26	7 51	8 31	9 39

Down	am	pm	pm	pm	pm	pm	pm	pm	pm	
Sundays										
Seaton Junction dep	1117	12 5	2 28	3 3	4 20	7 25	8 15	9 30	1020	.
Colyton	1121	12 9	2 32	3 7	4 24	7 29	8 19	9 34	1024	...
Colyford	1124	1212	2 35	3 10	4 27	7 32	8 24	9 39	1029	.
Seaton .... arr	1127	1215	2 38	3 13	4 30	7 35	8 28	9 43	1033	...

Up	am	am	pm	pm	pm	pm	pm	pm	pm
Sundays									
Seaton . .. .. dep	11 0	1135	2 8	2 43	3 35	7 2	7 52	9 5	9 50
Colyford	11 5	1140	2 13	2 48	3 40	7 7	7 57	9 12	9 57
Colyton	11 9	1144	2 17	2 52	3 44	7 11	8 1	9 17	10 2
Seaton Junction arr	1113	1148	2 21	2 56	3 48	7 15	8 5	9 21	10 6

A Through Carriages from Waterloo until 27th August **B** Through Carriages to Waterloo 2nd July to 27th August
F Fridays and Saturdays. **K** Saturdays only 2nd July to 27th August **SO** Saturdays only **SX** Mondays to Fridays
T Through Carriages to or from Waterloo **X** 5 minutes *earlier* on Saturdays **§** 1 minute later on Saturdays

Left: Services provided from the ex-LSWR main line junctions in July 1955.

Above: Ex-LSWR Radial tank 4-4-2T No 30584 arriving at Lyme Regis in June 1959. Three of the class survived well into BR days as they were very well suited to the demands of the branch line. *S. Creer*

Below centre: Ivatt Class 2 2-6-2T No 41291 arriving at Lyme Regis from Axminster at 12.54pm on 4 June 1963. *Ian Allan Library*

Bottom: Lyme Regis station with the 16.02 DMU departure to Axminster on 15 August 1964. Considerable demolition and rationalisation had been undertaken at the station, but the gas lamps remained. Today this view has been largely taken over by an industrial estate. *I. G. Holt*

19 North Devon necrosis

Ilfracombe with its ancient harbour on the North Devon coast was established as a holiday resort, with steamer services to South Wales, before the arrival of the railway. In July 1874 the Barnstaple & Ilfracombe Railway opened its 14½ mile route from Barnstaple. The line ran along the northern banks of the Taw estuary, before heading north from Braunton on a heavily graded section to the North Devon coast. The arrival of the railway resulted in the rapid growth of Ilfracombe. The LSWR operated the line from the start and between 1889 and 1891 the line was doubled, reflecting the increase of traffic on the route. Ilfracombe subsequently became a major holiday resort and through trains were run to the town from London and many other centres.

My first recollection of any train is on this line, when my father showed me in 1954, when I was five, two great engines struggling up the grade at a snail's pace, with my mother remonstrating, as mothers do, about the dangers of putting your head out of the window. Although I was hooked on trains from that date, I can remember my father bought a car, an Austin A30, at Combe Martin and we went home in that. The story is significant because, like millions of others, we deserted the railway for the road. Even in 1955 the seeds of the Beeching cuts were being sown.

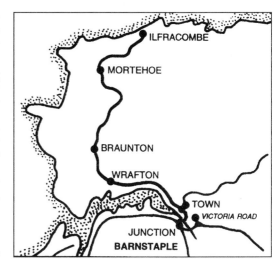

Below: Ilfracombe station being extended in LSWR days to provide additional protection from the rain and westerly gales that can on occasions strike this part of the North Devon coast. *E. Daniell*

I returned to Ilfracombe once more by train, this time in glorious sunshine as a 'Warship' class diesel growled up the same incline, but with a much shorter train. The diary records:

24 July 1968: From Barnstaple Junction station the line crosses the old town and over the River Taw which is followed for some time before the line turns inland and into a steep climb to Mortehoe. There are then falling grades as you travel through beautiful scenery to the coast. Ilfracombe station is gaunt, standing well above the town, and has masses of derelict sidings waiting for excursion trains that no longer run. On the return it is a very hard climb out of Ilfracombe and I wondered what would happen if the coupling snapped.

Passenger traffic could be light in the winter and the line was identified in the Beeching Report for closure. Yet Ilfracombe was regarded as one of the main Devon railheads and a considerable fight was put up to prevent the line's closure. However, its was all to no avail and the line closed to passengers in October 1970. Even then it was generally considered that such an important extension to the Barnstaple line would somehow be preserved, but after the failure of a preservation attempt the track was eventually lifted by 1975.

Above: To reach Ilfracombe the line was forced to cross the Taw estuary at Barnstaple on a curving metal bridge shown in this view taken from the 10.48 Ilfracombe to Exeter train on 30 July 1969. *J. H. Aston*

Left: The stone-built Barnstaple Town station remains, although the main building was unused when this view was taken in September 1995. The signalbox was in use as a small museum on the Lynton & Barnstaple Railway. *Author*

Above: The 2.10pm Ilfracombe to Waterloo train climbing to Mortehoe with 'M7' 0-4-4T No 30250 assisting unrebuilt 'West Country' Pacific No 34021 *Dartmoor* on 16 July 1955.
S. Creer

Left: Unrebuilt 'West Country' Pacific No 34070 on the 10.30 Ilfracombe to Waterloo train departs from Mortehoe on 9 September 1963.
J. Scrace

Below left: The difficult terrain just south of Ilfracombe involved the construction of tunnels at Slade. Originally a single line tunnel, the one to the left of this picture was added when the line was doubled and the new construction is still visible in this view taken in 1907.
F. E. Box

Top right: A similar view of the short Slade Tunnels in September 1995. One of the tunnels is now used as part of the footpath that follows the route of the line from Ilfracombe to Mortehoe.
Author

The station at Ilfracombe was not altogether easily accessible to the beach. It was also an exposed site and a locomotive was once blown round and round on the station's turntable by the force of the wind! The station has now been demolished and the site turned into an industrial area. At Barnstaple Town the stone-built station remains, but was unused in 1995. The signalbox also remains and is used as a museum for the Lynton and Barnstaple Railway. Much of the trackbed has been converted to a footpath. It has to be said that the demolition of the curving metal railway bridge at Barnstaple, which sat uncomfortably with the original 13th century stone bridge, has improved the environment of this part of the Taw estuary. Yet it remains hard to detect any other real benefit from the closure of this line.

Above: A 'Warship' diesel-hydraulic waits to depart from Ilfracombe on 24 July 1968. The sidings were unused and the signalling had been abandoned when this photograph was taken, but the economies were not to save the line.
Author

Left: Unrebuilt 'Battle of Britain' Pacific No 34072 *257 Squadron* marshals empty stock at Ilfracombe on 18 May 1959.
K. Cook

Left: Dereliction soon set in after closure, and this view of Ilfracombe station was taken in 1974. *D. Raby*

Below centre: The sad sight of Ilfracombe station being demolished in 1978. *D. Raby*

Bottom: The route out of Ilfracombe, by 1995, was heavily overgrown and today there are far more butterflies than passengers. The site of the station at Ilfracombe can just be seen in the distance by the chimney and is now an industrial estate. *Author*

20

Perchance it is not dead, but sleepeth

The 1ft 11½in narrow gauge Lynton & Barnstaple Railway ran from its terminus at Barnstaple Town, some 19½ miles, to Lynton on the North Devon coast. The railway was eventually opened after considerable difficulties in its construction in May 1898. The rugged terrain encountered crossing the shoulder of Exmoor resulted in construction costs being twice what had been anticipated, bankrupting the contractor.

Uniquely for an English narrow gauge line, the route was heavily engineered. Running in a northeasterly direction from Barnstaple along the valley of the River Yeo, the line included the eight-span 70ft high Chelfham Viaduct. The Lance Brook Viaduct which also had eight spans, but was of lesser height, and in all — about 80 other bridges. The route followed scenic and steep-sided valleys to Bratton Fleming before skirting Parracombe and Woody Bay where the line reached a summit of almost 1,000ft — the highest part of the Southern Railway — before eventually descending to a terminus at Lynton. Here the station was 250ft above the town, but a cliff passenger railway, which still remains open, was provided to the sea and Lynmouth.

Traffic was disappointing, but losses were not incurred until 1922. Indeed, the Southern Railway, which took over the following year, went out of its way to improve the service. It rather surprisingly provided a new Leeds-built Manning Wardle & Co 2-6-2T locomotive called *Lew*. This, the fifth engine for the line, was delivered in July 1925 and was very similar to the three older 2-6-2Ts. After incorporation within the Southern Railway the locomotives were turned out in Maunsell's olive green livery which made them look absolutely splendid.

The losses continued, though this was in part due to the recession of the 1930s, but in 1931 closure of the line was first mooted. It became clear that the Southern Railway, which promoted the route but also exercised financial prudence in all sections, was not prepared to invest in new track to keep the line going. Closure was announced for the end of September 1935.

Below: The attractive Manning Wardle-built No 188 2-6-2T *Lew*, seen here at Barnstaple Town station after delivery to the line in July 1925, in Southern Railway days. *Real Photos*

Above: On leaving Barnstaple Town the narrow gauge line curved away from the main line and crossed two roads, running alongside the River Yeo. At Pilton Causeway the level crossing gates were still in position many years after the closure of the line. *J. Palm*

Centre: After closure of the line the halt at Chelfham remained *in situ* for several years. *Ian Allan Library*

Left: A train coming off the viaduct at Chelfham in Southern Railway days. Note the Southern's early use of concrete with the telephone pole and fence posts. Concrete sleepers were also used on the narrow gauge line, well before they came into general use elsewhere. *F. E. Box*

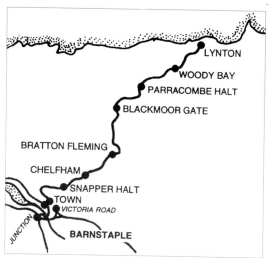

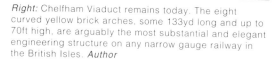

Right: Chelfham Viaduct remains today. The eight curved yellow brick arches, some 133yd long and up to 70ft high, are arguably the most substantial and elegant engineering structure on any narrow gauge railway in the British Isles. *Author*

Below: *Lew* No 188 takes water at Parracombe in 1934 in SR days. There was seldom any real shortage of water at this location. *A. B. MacLeod*

The last nine-coach train was filled to capacity. On departure from Lynton a band played Auld Lang Syne and the sad notes of the Last Post rang out over the station. The shrieking whistles of *Lew* and *Yeo* (the latter engine had worked the first train nearly 40 years before) and the exploding of detonators was repeated at all stations along the line. Evidence of the deep attachment for the little railway was clear from the vast numbers of onlookers that turned out to say a sad farewell. At Barnstaple about 1,000 people waited in the gloom and in rain to witness the arrival of the last train. A wreath at the station modified St Matthew's Gospel with the prophetic inscription 'Perchance it is not dead, but sleepeth'.

As it turned out this was in fact not to be the end of this charismatic railway. Apart from the many physical remains of the route, other items have been saved, including some rolling stock, such as the carriage from Snapper Halt and coach No 2 from the garden of Clannaborough rectory. The locomotive *Lew*, after working the demolition train escaped being scrapped, was overhauled in 1936 and shipped to a coffee plantation in Brazil. Here starts a real mystery. Although many suspect that the engine was scrapped in 1957, there have been alleged sightings of the locomotive, in a modified form, at locations throughout South America. If it does still exist, I am sure one day it will be returned to run on the Lynton & Barnstaple Railway.

In any event a new replica locomotive is being constructed at Boston Lodge on the Festiniog Railway. The locomotive will be of classic L&B Manning

Above: Parracombe station looking in the other direction, with a freight train passing through in SR days. Note the proud SR initials on the covered vans, even though they were unlikely to be consigned to any other company's lines.
Ian Allan Library

Left: Lynton & Lynmouth station, photographed in 1934. A compact, attractive and complete terminus with engine shed and signalling. *A. B. MacLeod*

Wardle design. There is growing pressure for reopening of this scenic route and the L&B Railway Association has already purchased part of the line. This very special sleeping beauty is undoubtedly destined to be resurrected from the dead.

Above: Lynton & Lynmouth station, as with others on the line, with their distinctive chalet-type roofs, remained largely intact when this view was taken in 1986. *Author*

Below: One of the concrete Lynton & Lynmouth station nameboards has been retained at Lynton. *J. Palm*

21

Lost on the Atlantic coast

The line from Halwill to Launceston was opened in July 1886, after which progress in this remote and often bleak part of Cornwall was slow. Services were extended to Tresmeer by the summer of 1892, Camelford by the following summer and to Wadebridge by June 1895, where the link to Padstow opened in March 1899. The line provided a 62¼-mile route to the Atlantic coast at Padstow from Okehampton. The 18½-mile Halwill to Bude line also ran to the Atlantic coast and with its concrete viaduct at Holsworthy was opened in August 1898. All the lines became part of a western arm of the LSWR. The Delabole slate quarry, the largest in the world, helped freight traffic. Fish traffic from the Atlantic at Bude and Padstow was also important, the latter port produced up to 1,000 wagonloads of fish a year in its heyday and a new fish dock was built by the Southern Railway in the 1930s.

In July 1925 the North Devon & Cornwall Junction Light Railway opened between Torrington and Halwill. The line was built with the involvement of Col H. F. Stephens and ran through a remote part of Devon. As with an earlier mineral line, which was utilised for part of the course of the new line, the main purpose of the link was to convey china clay. Consequently sharp curves and steep gradients were a feature of the route. The 20½-mile single line was one of the last substantial examples of a rural railway built in this country. The line was worked by the SR and, although notable for its use of typical SR distinctive concrete railway equipment, retained a separate identity until nationalisation.

At its opening, traffic was anticipated to merit the use of seven locomotives, but by 1953 traffic had declined and two were considered adequate. By 1959 even this number was not always necessary. Halwill still had periods of heavy operation on summer Saturdays, but passenger activity in any great amount was limited to a short summer season. Indeed,

passenger trains on the Torrington to Halwill line were noted for their lack of patronage.

The former Southern lines were transferred to the Western Region at the end of 1962. Services were quickly run down and in 1964 through trains to London and the famous 'Atlantic Coast Express' were ended. The Halwill-Torrington section was closed to

passengers in March 1965, having had a lifespan of just over 4 decades. Freight, however, remained on a section from Torrington to Meeth and the last train

Above left: Rebuilt 'Merchant Navy' Pacific No 35028 *Clan Line* awaits with the 'Atlantic Coast Express' headboard (ACE) at Waterloo. Not the original train, which ran for the last time on 5 September 1964, but a commemorative railway event held in October 1988. *Author*

Below left: At the other end of the line, Ivatt Class 2 2-6-2T Nos 41206 and 41291, back to back, leave the Halwill branch and enter Torrington. They are seen here on Saturday 27 March 1965 crossing the River Torridge with a special train, after the regular Torrington to Halwill passenger service had ended earlier that month. *Ian Allan Library*

Above: The bridge across the River Torridge remains in 1995 as part of the Tarka Trail. The footings of an earlier bridge from a mineral line that also crossed the river at this point can still just be seen below the water level in the river. *Author*

Right: As a reminder of the main traffic that once used the line, a china clay wagon and length of track have been preserved at Torrington station and are seen here in September 1995. The substantial stone-built station has been turned into a pub and restaurant containing many views of the local railways. *Author*

ran in 1983. The line from Halwill to Bude closed in October 1966, together with the sections west to Meldon Junction near Okehampton and to the coast at Wadebridge. Services remained between Padstow and Wadebridge until 1967. The diary records a trip over the former Southern lines in the southwest which have become known as the 'Withered Arm':

9 August 1966: Okehampton is a large station with loudspeakers and American-built locomotives at work nearby. The line to Bude was quite attractive, but the noticeable thing on this route was that there were very few passengers. The train from Halwill was also very little used and there was only one coach with a dozen or so passengers. Hardly anybody boarded the train until we arrived at Launceston, where I noted the Great Western station. The line then wound its way, through beautiful countryside, to Wadebridge which was quite a large station. I then joined the train from Padstow to Bodmin Road which again was a single coach, full of girl guides. Only one person alighted at a halt that provides connection for Bodmin North and the train waited only a short time before reaching Bodmin General. At Bodmin Road a 'Warship' diesel came along and provided a lively performance with its very short train.

There have been many losses on the Atlantic coast. Not only the numerous shipwrecks on the rugged rocks, but also the fish stocks, are today, like the railway, sadly much depleted. Yet many traces of the 'Withered Arm' lines remain. At Launceston a section is used by a narrow gauge steam tourist railway. Other parts are now footpaths and many of the distinctive station buildings are still to be found along the lost lines to the Atlantic coast.

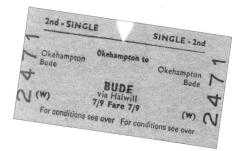

Above: Ivatt Class 2 No 41283 pauses at Hatherleigh with the 4pm Torrington to Halwill train on 14 August 1963. *P. Paye*

Below: The site of Yarde Halt in August 1995. The former halt now lies on part of the Tarka Trail which provides a walking link between Bideford and Hatherleigh. *Author*

Right: A Southern Railway poster, painted by A. Tripp, with a view of Bude's sandy beach. Bude is now about 35 miles from the nearest main line station. *Courtesy NRM*

BUDE

ILLUSTRATED GUIDE FROM CLERK TO THE COUNCIL. DEPT 'P'. COUNCIL OFFICES. BUDE

SOUTHERN RAILWAY

SOUTHERN RAILWAY ADVERTISING

Above: Halwill was a considerable junction with four lines converging on the station. Note the clock and the particularly tall booking office doors. *F. Crudass*

Left: The former LSWR signal-box at Launceston station, viewed from the train on a wet 9 August 1966. *Author*

Above right: Class T9 4-4-0 No 30709 with the train for Padstow at Egloskerry station on 21 April 1960. *R. Joanes*

Left: Egloskerry station buildings and one of the concrete nameboards still remained *in situ* in September 1995. *Author*

Below left: A single carriage 'bubblecar' on the 14.25 Wadebridge to Halwill service pauses at Otterham station on 1 July 1966. The stone-built station buildings remain largely unchanged today and are of a similar design to many others on the North Cornwall line. *J. Spencer Gilks*

Right: The concrete sign at Camelford with its indication that the station was also for Boscastle and Tintagel on the Atlantic coast, viewed here from the train on 9 August 1966. *Author*

Below: 'West Country' Pacific No 34004 *Yeovil*, in the early 1950s, approaching St Kew Highway, north of Wadebridge, with a down stopping passenger train. *B. Butt*

Above: The 11.00 'Atlantic Coast Express' (ACE) Waterloo to Padstow train, hauled by 'Battle of Britain' Pacific No 34054 *Lord Beaverbrook*, is seen here crossing Little Petherick Creek Bridge near Padstow, in May 1964, before through services were withdrawn. The bridge remains and this part of the line is currently in use as a footpath as part of the Camel Trail. *S. C. Nash*

Below: Timetable showing the very limited service provided between Halwill and Torrington in July 1955.

Above right: The station house at Padstow remains in use as a custom house, as this view taken in August 1995 shows. The stone-built building is of solid and distinctive design, similar to other stations on the North Cornwall line. *Author*

Below right: The western arm of the Southern's empire. The furthest part of the Southern from Waterloo was at Padstow — the green railings and platform shown here in August 1995 still survive. Perhaps they are awaiting the day when trains will return. *Author*

Table 43 **HALWILL, HATHERLEIGH and TORRINGTON**

Miles	Week Days only	am	am SX	am SO	pm SX	pm
	Halwill .. .. .. dep	..	**1040**	**1052**	..	**6 30**
3	Hole	....	1049	11 1	....	6 39
7¾	Hatherleigh	..	11 7	1119	..	6 57
10	Meeth Halt	....	1120	1132	....	7 8
12¾	Petrockstow	7 55	1130	1142	4 37	7 18
14¾	Dunsbear Halt	8 4	1140	1152	4 46	7 28
16	Yarde Halt	8 10	1145	1157	4 52	7 34
18¾	Watergate Halt	8 24	1159	1211	5 6	7 48
20½	**Torrington** .. .. arr	**8 32**	**12 6**	**1218**	**5 14**	**7 56**

Miles	Week Days only	am	am	pm SX	pm SO
	Torrington .. .. dep	**6 25**	**8 52**	**4 0**	**4 40**
1¾	Watergate Halt	6 32	8 59	4 7	4 47
4½	Yarde Halt	6 46	9 13	4 20	5 1
5¾	Dunsbear Halt	6 52	9 18	4 25	5 6
7¾	Petrockstow	7† 4	9 28	4 34	5 16
10½	Meeth Halt	....	9 38	4 44	5 26
12¾	Hatherleigh	..	9 48	4 54	5 36
17½	Hole	....	10 8	5 13	5 56
20½	**Halwill** .. .. .. arr	..	**1018**	**5 23**	**6 6**

SO Saturdays only **SX** Mondays to Fridays † Arrival

117

22 Camel freight trains

Cornwall's tin mines were pioneers in the use of steam for pumping engines. Equally the Bodmin & Wadebridge Railway was an early steam line that ran from the navigable reaches of the River Camel at Wadebridge, up the wooded and twisting valley of the river to Wenfordbridge, with lines also to Bodmin and Ruthernbridge. Originally built mainly to carry ore for shipment, the railway opened between Wadebridge and Dunmere in July 1834 and throughout in the latter part of that year. It was taken over by the LSWR, but not connected to the rest of the railway system until a branch from Bodmin Road, on the Great Western main line, opened as far as Boscarne Junction in September 1888 and the North Cornwall Railway opened to Wadebridge in June 1895.

The section from Boscarne Junction to Wenfordbridge was a freight-only route and the main rail traffic to develop was powdered china clay from the Wenford Dries works, where wet clay is dried. The eventual destination was the harbour at Fowey. The sight of china clay freight trains winding along the steeply graded and curved track in the valley of the River Camel was an attractive feature of this part of Cornwall. Even after the end of steam, the introduction in the mid-1970s of tent-like tarpaulin-covered 'clay hood' wagons provided a particularly distinctive look to the services.

Passenger services ran between Bodmin Road, via Bodmin General, to Wadebridge and Padstow and between Bodmin North and Wadebridge and Padstow. Steam-hauled passenger services ended in 1963, but DMU services continued until January 1967. The track west of Wadebridge was the first to be lifted, but that from Boscarne Junction to Wadebridge followed after closure of this section to regular freight traffic in 1978. Freight trains to Ruthernbridge ceased as far back as 1933, but freight remained on the Bodmin Road to Boscarne Junction and Wenfordbridge section for another 50 years until September 1983.

Below: A Beattie 2-4-0 Well Tank No 30587 shunts in the substantial yard at Wadebridge on 22 September 1959. *P. Treloar*

Right: The stone-built Wadebridge station and goods shed are well preserved. Part of the station has been converted into the John Betjeman centre. *Author*

Below right: A Beattie Well Tank No 30585 runs past Boscarne Junction signalbox and an ex-London and South Western Railway signal during shunting of a Wenfordbridge train. *P. Treloar*

This was not to be the end of the story. Cornwall's first standard gauge preserved railway opened from the main line junction at Bodmin Road, now renamed Bodmin Parkway, to the Bodmin General terminus in 1989. The Bodmin & Wenford Railway has become the home to an impressive collection of rolling stock. Indeed freight ran over the preserved route from 1989 until the end of the Speedlink network in July 1991. Even then freight services continued on china clay workings until rises in charges in 1992 led to contracts not being renewed.

Rails on the tortuous route from Boscarne Junction to Wenfordbridge have been lifted and much of the trackbed, together with that to Padstow, made

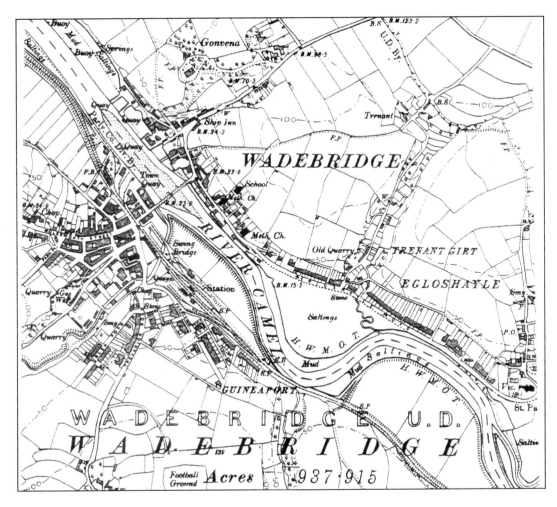

into a long distance path known as the Camel Trail. However, it was recognised that use of the line to the Wenfordbridge clay works would cut drastically the numbers of heavy lorries running over narrow roads in the area. Proposals encompass reopening the line from Boscarne Junction to Wenfordbridge for china clay traffic, and there is also backing for regular passenger services between Bodmin Parkway, Bodmin General and Boscarne Junction. At Boscarne Junction the trackbed, still largely clear of obstruction, heads for Wadebridge where the station has been restored as the John Betjeman Centre. Beyond Wadebridge is the lure of Padstow. Perhaps one day Betjeman's ghost will travel here once again by train.

Above: Map of Wadebridge station 1908.
Crown Copyright

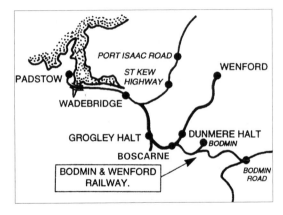

Above: Part of the former line from Dunmere Junction to Bodmin North station has been turned into a connecting link to the Camel Trail, as this view near Bodmin North station taken in August 1995 shows. The former North station site has been redeveloped as a supermarket. Bodmin General remains in the town, used by the Bodmin & Wenford Railway. *Author*

Below: A Beattie Well Tank No 30587 takes the Wenfordbridge line at Dunmere Junction with a freight from Wadebridge on 7 August 1962. *W. Sumner*

Left: A Beattie Well Tank No 30587 (old LSWR No 298) is flagged across the road by Dunmere siding to pick up a wagon, which it will then shunt back across the road, before continuing its route to Wenfordbridge from Wadebridge with a freight train in the 1950s. *J. Haydon*

Below centre: The crossing near Dunmere siding, viewed here in August 1995, still retains the rails in the road, awaiting a reopening of the line to the Wenfordbridge clay works. *Author*

Bottom: The 10.30am Wadebridge to Wenfordbridge freight train, in the wooded Camel valley near Penhargard, hauled by a Beattie Well Tank No 30585, on 3 September 1953. *S. C. Nash*

Above: The terminus at Wenfordbridge: a Beattie Well Tank No 30585 is engaged in marshalling the train, principally of covered loaded china clay wagons, for the return journey. This view was taken on 22 September 1959. *P. Treloar*

Below: Part of the Camel Trail near Wenfordbridge, viewed here in August 1995. *Author*

23 ABC – Back to the future

A-Alps

As the network of lines began to develop, the Mid-Hants Railway opened, in October 1865, a route which linked the main line north of Winchester with Alton. Although built to main line standards, the route was heavily graded in parts and was essentially secondary in nature. Nevertheless it served for many years as a useful diversionary line from London to Southampton.

By 1937 electrification reached Alton, but with no plans to continue to Winchester, a change at Alton for most trains meant that passengers using the line were inconvenienced. In 1957 efforts were made to enhance the service and steam was replaced by an hourly diesel service. Patronage increased, economies were made and my diary noted that in 1967 tickets were issued on the train. However, the Beeching Report had identified the line for the with-

Right: The 10.52 Southampton to Alton train formed of DEMU No 1122 departs from Itchen Abbas on the still closed section of the Mid-Hants Railway. This view was taken on 7 January 1968. *J. H. Bird*

Below: A rebuilt 'Merchant Navy' Pacific No 35008 *Orient Line* heading the 10.30 Waterloo to Weymouth train between Alton and Medstead on 1 May 1966. The train was diverted 'over the Alps' due to engineering works on the main line. *W. Sumner*

drawal of passenger services and the first closure notices appeared in 1967. There was considerable opposition which led to postponement, but the line was eventually closed in February 1973.

There were immediate plans to reopen and purchase the line, but unfortunately the first share issue failed; nevertheless the second was successful and the line was purchased from Alresford to Alton. Meanwhile in 1976 British Rail tore up the track between Alton and Ropley; therefore it was a very great credit to the preserved railway when the track was relaid over this steeply-graded section, sometimes known as the Alps. Today the line operates 'over the Alps' from Alresford to Alton. With an eye to the future in the 1980s British Rail provided, as in the past, interchange facilities for the line with electric trains at Alton.

B-Bluebell

The line from East Grinstead to Culver Junction, near Lewes, opened in August 1882 and a link from

Above: Preserved ex-LBSCR Class E4 0-6-2T *Birch Grove* on the rear of a London Victoria to Sheffield Park excursion, passing Ardingly on 31 March 1963. If the past is any guide to the future, the long-term prospect for this closed line, which links to the Bluebell Railway, may well be promising. *S. C. Nash*

Below: The 11.33am Lewes to East Grinstead train leaving West Hoathly on 6 October 1956 headed by an ex-LBSCR C2x 0-6-0 No 32442. After an absence of many years the Bluebell Railway returned passenger services once again to this section of line during 1995. *R. Taylor*

Table 47 LONDON, ALTON, ALRESFORD, EASTLEIGH and SOUTHAMPTON

Miles	Down	Week Days													Sundays			
		am	am Mondays to Fridays	am Saturdays only	am	pm Mondays to Fridays	pm Saturdays only	pm	pm	pm	pm Mondays to Fridays	pm Saturdays only	pm	pm Mondays to Fridays	am	am	pm	pm
	Waterloo 70 .. .. dep	**6 25**	**725**	**7 28**	**10f27**	**1257**	**1 2**	**2f27**	**3f27**	**4K27**	**5 57**	**5 57**	**657**	**7 57**	**7 25**	**1027**	**327**	**6 57**
—	**Alton** .... dep	**7 53**	**855**	**9 20**	**12 5**	**2 30**	**2 30**	**4 10**	**5 5**	**6 2**	**7 25**	**7 30**	**840**	**9 35**	**8 55**	**12 5**	**455**	**8 20**
51¼	Medstead and Four Marks	8 5	9 7	9 32	12 17	2 42	2 42	4 22	5 17	6 14	7 37	7 42	852	9 47	9 7	1217	5 7	8 32
54¼	Ropley	8 11	912	9 38	12 23	2 48	2 48	4 28	5 23	6 19	7 43	7 47	858	9 53	9 12	1222	512	8 38
57	Alresford	8C18	917	9 43	12 29	2 54	2J58	4C34	5B39	6C25	7G52	7C54	9 2	9 57	9 17	1227	517	8 43
60¼	Itchen Abbas	8 24	923	9 49	12 33	3 0	3 4	4 40	5 45	6 31	7 58	8 0	9 8	10 3	9 23	1233	523	8 50
65¾	Winchester City .. .. .. arr	8 35	935	10 1	12 44	3 13	3 16	4V51	5 56	6 42	8 10	8 12	919	1014	9 33	1244	534	9 2
69	28 Shawford .... arr	8 42	941	10 7	12 50	3 19	3 22	4V57	6 2	..	8 15	8 17	926	..	9 39	1250	.	9 8
72¾	28 Eastleigh .. .. „	8 50	949	1015	12 58	3 27	3 30	5V 3	6 9	....	8 23	8 25	934	....	9 47	1258	...	9 16
75	28 Swaythling .... „	..	.	..	..	..	..	5 13	..	..	..	..	.	..	9b58	..	.	9 23
76¼	28 St. Denys .. .. „	....	...	....	....	....	....	5 17	....	....	....	....	...	....	10b 2	....	...	9 27
77¼	28 Northam .... „	..	.	..	..	..	..	5 21	..	..	..	..	.	..	..	..	.	..
78¼	28 **Southampton Terminus**. „	....	...	....	....	....	....	**5 24**	....	....	....	....	...	....	**10b 8**	....	...	**9 33**

Miles	Up	Week Days														Sundays			
		am	am	am Mons. to Fris.	am Saturdays only	pm Saturdays only	pm Mondays to Fridays	pm Mondays to Fridays	pm Saturdays only	pm	pm	pm	pm Saturdays only	pm Mondays to Fridays	pm Mondays to Fridays	am	am	pm	pm
—	28 **Southampton Terminus**. dep	..	..		..	..			.	..	..	**523**	**652**	**658**	**7 40**	..	..	..	..
¾	28 Northam .... „	....	....		....	....			....	....	....	526	655	7 1	7 43	....	....	....	....
1¾	28 St. Denys .. .. „	..	..		..	..			.	..	..	530	659	7 5	7 48	..	..	..	..
3¼	28 Swaythling .... „	....	....		....	....			....	....	....	534	7 3	7 9	7 51	....	....	....	....
5¼	28 Eastleigh .. .. „	6 35	7 42	1016	1036	1 5	1 15	2 20	224	3 59	4 55	544	716	715	7 58	7 45	1046	3 42	..
9¼	28 Shawford .... „	6 42	7 49	1023	..	1 12	1 22	2 27	231	4 6	5 2	553	724	722	8 6	7 52	1053	3 49	....
12¼	Winchester City .. .. .. dep	6 50	7 58	1032	1051	1 20	1 29	2 34	238	4 14	5 9	6 4	732	730	8 14	7 59	11 0	3 56	7 27
17¾	Itchen Abbas	7 2	8 10	1044	11 5	1 32	1 41	2 46	250	4 26	5 21	618	745	742	8 27	8 11	1112	4 8	7 38
21¼	Alresford	7 9	8 17	1051	1112	1 39	1 48	2C55	257	4C35	5 28	625	753	750	8 34	8 18	1119	4 15	7 45
24	Ropley	7 16	8 24	1058	1119	1 46	1 55	3 2	3 4	4 42	5 35	632	8 0	757	8 41	8 25	1126	4 22	7 53
27	Medstead and Four Marks	7 25	8 33	11 7	1128	1 55	2 4	3 11	312	4 51	5 44	640	8 9	8 6	8 50	8 34	1135	4 31	8 1
31¼	**Alton** .... arr	**7 34**	**8 42**	**1116**	**1137**	**2 4**	**2 13**	**3 20**	**321**	**5 0**	**5 52**	**649**	**818**	**815**	**9 2**	**8 43**	**1144**	**4 41**	**8 10**
78¼	**Waterloo 70** .. .. arr	**8a57**	**9L57**	**1246**	**1 23**	**3 45**	**3 46**	**4 46**	**445**	**6 46**	**7a16**	**816**	**946**	**946**	**10d46**	**1016**	**1 16**	**6 16**	**9H46**

a 2 minutes later on Saturdays
B Arr 5 27 pm
b Commences 3rd July
C Arr 2 minutes *earlier*
d 10 41 pm on Tuesdays, Wednesdays and Thursdays 26th July to 25th Aug.
f 3 minutes later on Saturdays
G Arr 4 minutes *earlier*
H 9 40 pm 24th July to 28th August
J Arr 5 minutes *earlier*
K Dep 4 47 pm Mondays to Fridays
L Arr 10 17 am on Saturdays
V 1 minute later on Saturdays

For OTHER TRAINS between London and Southampton, see Table 28

Above: Timetable showing the limited and unbalanced through service using the Mid-Hants line in July 1955.

Right: Class M7 No 30060 and set 385 arrive at Corfe Castle with the 12.16pm from Wareham on 6 September 1955. The vintage signalbox was demolished in the autumn of 1956, but the ornate stone station buildings remain. *J. H. Aston*

Horsted Keynes to Haywards Heath opened in September of the following year. Although the lines afforded a diversionary route to Brighton, after World War 2 local traffic diminished and the East Grinstead to Lewes route finally closed in March 1958. The line from Horsted Keynes to Haywards Heath, which had been electrified in the 1930s, closed in October 1963, although it was used for a little longer for stock transfers to the Bluebell Railway.

The Bluebell Railway was the first standard gauge BR passenger preserved line. When this futuristic idea was first put forward many thought the whole concept highly implausible. Yet in 1960 a section of track from Sheffield Park to near Horsted Keynes was in operation. By 1968 the line had been secured and the railway was sole user of Horsted Keynes. The line today is vastly different from that of the 1960s. It has gone from strength to strength, conveying more passengers than ever. The line is set to run once again to East Grinstead. Is it therefore any more implausible to suggest that it may well also, one day in the future, return to Haywards Heath?

C-Corfe Castle

The stubborn refusal of Corfe Castle to surrender to Cromwell in the English Civil War perhaps provided a lesson for the stubborn refusal of the Wareham, Worgret Junction, to Swanage line to die. Opened in May 1885, the route was not identified by Beeching for closure. Nevertheless it was finally closed to passengers in January 1972 after a five-year battle with protesters. A campaign to reopen the branch began as soon as it closed. The line has made a comeback across the Isle of Purbeck from Swanage to Corfe Castle and Norden. At Norden the railway now provides a 'park and ride' facility which will help in the future to protect the environment of Corfe from cars.

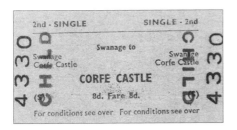

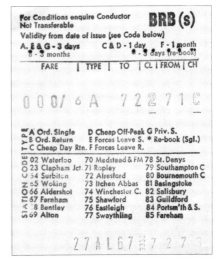

Today, as in the past, it is possible once again to reach Swanage by train. The diary states:

23 July 1968: A full train left for Wareham, it was the new Southern Region diesel-electric set, and very smart. The Wareham to Swanage train left only partly filled and it was a pleasant ride. I saw Corfe Castle, but the town was inundated with cars and did not look as romantic as Hamilton Ellis's painting of LSWR days. Swanage station was also quite large, but now reduced to a single track, although it abounded with porters, foremen and so on.

In conclusion, without the hard work, dedication and financial investment of countless volunteers the many well-known preserved lines could not have become so magnificent as they are today. Although they capture a glimpse of the past, as with rail travel in general, they are likely to expand and grow from strength to strength in the future. The next time you fancy some 'southern comfort' turn to the the *European Railway Atlas: British Isles,* published by Ian Allan Ltd, and plan your trip back to the future!

Above: Unrebuilt 'West Country' Pacific No 34023 *Blackmore Vale* leaves Corfe Castle for Swanage after a photographic stop on an LCGB tour in 1967. A view from the past which will be repeated in the future.
A. McIntyre

Left: Back again, passengers return to the train at Corfe Castle in September 1995. When the train service reopened to the station in August 1995 it was estimated that about 20,000 passengers used the Norden, Corfe and Swanage line in the first week.
Author